THE ENCYCLOPEDIA OF PSYCHOACTIVE DRUGS

SERIES 1

SERIES 2

DRINKING, DRIVING & DRUGS

GENERAL EDITOR
Professor Solomon H. Snyder, M.D.

*Distinguished Service Professor of
Neuroscience, Pharmacology, and Psychiatry at
The Johns Hopkins University School of Medicine*

•

ASSOCIATE EDITOR
Professor Barry L. Jacobs, Ph.D.

*Program in Neuroscience, Department of Psychology,
Princeton University*

•

SENIOR EDITORIAL CONSULTANT
Joann Rodgers

*Deputy Director, Office of Public Affairs at
The Johns Hopkins Medical Institutions*

THE ENCYCLOPEDIA OF PSYCHOACTIVE DRUGS

SERIES 2

DRINKING, DRIVING & DRUGS

JEAN MCBEE KNOX

CHELSEA HOUSE PUBLISHERS
NEW YORK • PHILADELPHIA

EDITOR-IN-CHIEF: Nancy Toff
EXECUTIVE EDITOR: Remmel T. Nunn
MANAGING EDITOR: Karyn Gullen Browne
COPY CHIEF: Juliann Barbato
PICTURE EDITOR: Adrian G. Allen
ART DIRECTOR: Giannella Garrett
MANUFACTURING MANAGER: Gerald Levine

Staff for DRINKING, DRIVING, AND DRUGS:

SENIOR EDITOR: Jane Larkin Crain
ASSOCIATE EDITOR: Paula Edelson
ASSISTANT EDITOR: Laura-Ann Dolce
EDITORIAL ASSISTANT: Susan DeRosa
COPY EDITOR: Karen Hammonds
DEPUTY COPY CHIEF: Ellen Scordato
ASSOCIATE PICTURE EDITOR: Juliette Dickstein
PICTURE RESEARCHER: Nisa Rauschenberg
DESIGNER: Victoria Tomaselli
DESIGN ASSISTANT: Ghila Krajzman
PRODUCTION COORDINATOR: Joseph Romano
COVER ILLUSTRATION: Taurus Photos © John Lidington

3 5 7 9 8 6 4 2

Library of Congress Cataloging in Publication Data

Knox, Jean.
   Drinking, Driving, and Drugs.
   (The Encyclopedia of psychoactive drugs. Series 2)
   Bibliography: p.
   Includes index.
   1. Youth—United States—Alcohol use—Juvenile literature. 2. Youth—United
States—Drug use—Juvenile literature. 3. Juvenile automobile drivers—United
States—Juvenile literature. 4. Drinking and traffic accidents—United States—
Juvenile literature. [1. Drunk driving. 2. Drug abuse. 3. Alcohol]
I. Title. II. Series.
HV5135.K58   1987   363.1'251   87-27733

ISBN 1-55546-231-6
    0-7910-0783-9 (pbk.)

CONTENTS

Drunk driving has reached epidemic proportions, endangering the lives of everyone on the road. Safeguarding the nation's highways against this menace could save tens of thousands of lives a year.

In the Mainstream
of American Life

One of the legacies of the social upheaval of the 1960s is that psychoactive drugs have become part of the mainstream of American life. Schools, homes, and communities cannot be "drug proofed." There is a demand for drugs — and the supply is plentiful. Social norms have changed and drugs are not only available—they are everywhere.

But where efforts to curtail the supply of drugs and outlaw their use have had tragically limited effects on demand, it may be that education has begun to stem the rising tide of drug abuse among young people and adults alike.

Over the past 25 years, as drugs have become an increasingly routine facet of contemporary life, a great many teenagers have adopted the notion that drug taking was somehow a right or a privilege or a necessity. They have done so, however, without understanding the consequences of drug use during the crucial years of adolescence.

The teenage years are few in the total life cycle, but critical in the maturation process. During these years adolescents face the difficult tasks of discovering their identity, clarifying their sexual roles, asserting their independence, learning to cope with authority, and searching for goals that will give their lives meaning.

Drugs rob adolescents of precious time, stamina, and health. They interrupt critical learning processes, sometimes forever. Teenagers who use drugs are likely to withdraw increasingly into themselves, to "cop out" at just the time when they most need to reach out and experience the world.

A well-stocked bar at a private party. The use of alcohol is routine at social gatherings, and it is likely that many who overindulge will get behind the wheel of a car before their night out is over.

Fortunately, as a recent Gallup poll shows, young people are beginning to realize this, too. They themselves label drugs their most important problem. In the last few years, moreover, the climate of tolerance and ignorance surrounding drugs has been changing.

Adolescents as well as adults are becoming aware of mounting evidence that every race, ethnic group, and class is vulnerable to drug dependency.

Recent publicity about the cost and failure of drug rehabilitation efforts; dangerous drug use among pilots, air traffic controllers, star athletes, and Hollywood celebrities; and drug-related accidents, suicides, and violent crime have focused the public's attention on the need to wage an all-out war on drug abuse before it seriously undermines the fabric of society itself.

The anti-drug message is getting stronger and there is evidence that the message is beginning to get through to adults and teenagers alike.

The Encyclopedia of Psychoactive Drugs hopes to play a part in the national campaign now underway to educate young people about drugs. Series 1 provides clear and comprehensive discussions of common psychoactive substances, outlines their psychological and physiological effects on the mind and body, explains how they "hook" the user, and separates fact from myth in the complex issue of drug abuse.

Whereas Series 1 focuses on specific drugs, such as nicotine or cocaine, Series 2 confronts a broad range of both social and physiological phenomena. Each volume addresses the ramifications of drug use and abuse on some aspect of human experience: social, familial, cultural, historical, and physical. Separate volumes explore questions about the effects of drugs on brain chemistry and unborn children; the use and abuse of painkillers; the relationship between drugs and sexual behavior, sports, and the arts; drugs and disease; the role of drugs in history; and the sophisticated drugs now being developed in the laboratory that will profoundly change the future.

Each book in the series is fully illustrated and is tailored to the needs and interests of young readers. The more adolescents know about drugs and their role in society, the less likely they are to misuse them.

Joann Rodgers
Senior Editorial Consultant

In this 17th-century engraving, tipsy winemakers test their product "on location" in a wine cellar. Excessive consumption of alcohol has been a feature of Western civilization for centuries.

INTRODUCTION

The Gift of Wizardry Use and Abuse

JACK H. MENDELSON, M.D.
NANCY K. MELLO, Ph.D.
Alcohol and Drug Abuse Research Center
Harvard Medical School—McLean Hospital

Dorothy to the Wizard:

"I think you are a very bad man," said Dorothy.
"Oh no, my dear; I'm really a very good man; but I'm a very bad Wizard."
—from THE WIZARD OF OZ

Man is endowed with the gift of wizardry, a talent for discovery and invention. The discovery and invention of substances that change the way we feel and behave are among man's special accomplishments, and, like so many other products of our wizardry, these substances have the capacity to harm as well as to help. Psychoactive drugs can cause profound changes in the chemistry of the brain and other vital organs, and although their legitimate use can relieve pain and cure disease, their abuse leads in a tragic number of cases to destruction.

Consider alcohol — available to all and yet regarded with intense ambivalence from biblical times to the present day. The use of alcoholic beverages dates back to our earliest ancestors. Alcohol use and misuse became associated with the worship of gods and demons. One of the most powerful Greek gods was Dionysus, lord of fruitfulness and god of wine. The Romans adopted Dionysus but changed his name to Bacchus. Festivals and holidays associated with Bacchus celebrated the harvest and the origins of life. Time has blurred the images of the Bacchanalian festival, but the theme of drunkenness as a major part of celebration has survived the pagan gods and remains a familiar part of modern society. The term "Bacchanalian Festival" conveys a more appealing image than "drunken orgy" or "pot party," but whatever the label, drinking alcohol is a form of drug use that results in addiction for millions.

The fact that many millions of other people can use alcohol in moderation does not mitigate the toll this drug takes on society as a whole. According to reliable estimates, one out of every ten Americans develops a serious alcohol-related problem sometime in his or her lifetime. In addition, automobile accidents caused by drunken drivers claim the lives of tens of thousands every year. Many of the victims are gifted young people, just starting out in adult life. Hospital emergency rooms abound with patients seeking help for alcohol-related injuries.

Who is to blame? Can we blame the many manufacturers who produce such an amazing variety of alcoholic beverages? Should we blame the educators who fail to explain the perils of intoxication, or so exaggerate the dangers of drinking that no one could possibly believe them? Are friends to blame — those peers who urge others to "drink more and faster," or the macho types who stress the importance of being able to "hold your liquor"? Casting blame, however, is hardly constructive, and pointing the finger is a fruitless way to deal with the problem. Alcoholism and drug abuse have few culprits but many victims. Accountability begins with each of us, every time we choose to use or misuse an intoxicating substance.

It is ironic that some of man's earliest medicines, derived from natural plant products, are used today to poison and to intoxicate. Relief from pain and suffering is one of society's many continuing goals. Over 3,000 years ago, the Therapeutic Papyrus of Thebes, one of our earliest written records, gave instructions for the use of opium in the treatment of pain. Opium, in the form of its major derivative, morphine, and similar compounds, such as heroin, have also been used by many to induce changes in mood and feeling. Another example of man's misuse of a natural substance is the coca leaf, which for centuries was used by the Indians of Peru to reduce fatigue and hunger. Its modern derivative, cocaine, has important medical use as a local anesthetic. Unfortunately, its

14

increasing abuse in the 1980s clearly has reached epidemic proportions.

The purpose of this series is to explore in depth the psychological and behavioral effects that psychoactive drugs have on the individual, and also, to investigate the ways in which drug use influences the legal, economic, cultural, and even moral aspects of societies. The information presented here (and in other books in this series) is based on many clinical and laboratory studies and other observations by people from diverse walks of life.

Over the centuries, novelists, poets, and dramatists have provided us with many insights into the sometimes seductive but ultimately problematic aspects of alcohol and drug use. Physicians, lawyers, biologists, psychologists, and social scientists have contributed to a better understanding of the causes and consequences of using these substances. The authors in this series have attempted to gather and condense all the latest information about drug use and abuse. They have also described the sometimes wide gaps in our knowledge and have suggested some new ways to answer many difficult questions.

One such question, for example, is how do alcohol and drug problems get started? And what is the best way to treat them when they do? Not too many years ago, alcoholics and drug abusers were regarded as evil, immoral, or both. It is now recognized that these persons suffer from very complicated diseases involving deep psychological and social problems. To understand how the disease begins and progresses, it is necessary to understand the nature of the substance, the behavior of addicts, and the characteristics of the society or culture in which they live.

Although many of the social environments we live in are very similar, some of the most subtle differences can strongly influence our thinking and behavior. Where we live, go to school and work, whom we discuss things with — all influence our opinions about drug use and misuse. Yet we also share certain commonly accepted beliefs that outweigh any differences in our attitudes. The authors in this series have tried to identify and discuss the central, most crucial issues concerning drug use and misuse.

Despite the increasing sophistication of the chemical substances we create in the laboratory, we have a long way to go in our efforts to make these powerful drugs work for us rather than against us.

The volumes in this series address a wide range of timely questions. What influence has drug use had on the arts? Why do so many of today's celebrities and star athletes use drugs, and what is being done to solve this problem? What is the relationship between drugs and crime? What is the physiological basis for the power drugs can hold over us? These are but a few of the issues explored in this far-ranging series.

Educating people about the dangers of drugs can go a long way towards minimizing the desperate consequences of substance abuse for individuals and society as a whole. Luckily, human beings have the resources to solve even the most serious problems that beset them, once they make the commitment to do so. As one keen and sensitive observer, Dr. Lewis Thomas, has said,

> There is nothing at all absurd about the human condition. We matter. It seems to me a good guess, hazarded by a good many people who have thought about it, that we may be engaged in the formation of something like a mind for the life of this planet. If this is so, we are still at the most primitive stage, still fumbling with language and thinking, but infinitely capacitated for the future. Looked at this way, it is remarkable that we've come as far as we have in so short a period, really no time at all as geologists measure time. We are the newest, youngest, and the brightest thing around.

DRINKING, DRIVING, & DRUGS

Motor-vehicle accidents are responsible for 45% of all teenage deaths. Among those killed, at least 60% had been drinking. Sixteen-year-old drivers account for 40% of all single car alcohol-related crashes.

Imagine a crowd of 44,000 people in the stands at a World Series or Super Bowl game. A television camera scans the individual faces — some exuberant, some anxious — all sports fans out for a good time.

As many people as are in that crowd will die in highway accidents this year. More than half of those accidents will involve alcohol, alone or in combination with other drugs. A disproportionate number of the dead will be young, between the ages of 15 and 24. One group, 16 year olds, will be in 40% of all the single-car, alcohol-related crashes.

The life expectancy of every age group in this country has risen in the past two decades, with the notable exception of teenagers. Motor-vehicle accidents are largely to blame, accounting for 45% of teenage deaths. Other accidents, such as falls or drowning, account for only 13%.

Among fatally injured teenage drivers, at least 60% had been drinking prior to their crash. In 1984 alone, 9,000 people between the ages of 15 and 24 were killed in alcohol-related crashes. Another 220,000 were injured, many maimed for life.

Driving while intoxicated (DWI), however, is not an isolated teenage problem. Alcohol is the number-one killer on the road; despite the frightening statistics, a widespread belief persists among all age groups in this country that the risk of DWI is worth taking. A 1985 Gallup poll showed that two-thirds of all Americans are drinkers, and almost one-third admit to having driven after drinking alcohol. A parallel survey of American business executives shows that 80% have driven while drunk. The U.S. Department of Transportation estimates that about 10% of all drivers on a weekend night are legally intoxicated. The majority of those drunk drivers somehow are making their way home alive.

But those who never make it home are too often teenagers. Young people between the ages of 15 and 24 represent only 20% of the licensed drivers in this country, yet they are involved in 42% of all fatal alcohol-related crashes. According to the Department of Health and Human Services, three-quarters of all teenagers are drinking by the age of sixteen. If they have been drinking, young drivers are three times more likely to have a fatal crash than are older drivers. The untimely deaths of these drivers shatter families, friends, and even entire communities with grief and seem to mock the future of all young people. If the tragedy of drunk driving affects all ages, why are young people so often the victims?

Alcohol and Adolescents

Often, the first reason given by adolescents themselves to drink and use other drugs is peer pressure. "Macho" recklessness and approval of excessive drinking on the part of boys, who compose the majority of drinking teenage drivers,

Approximately 44,000 people, about the same number who attend a World Series or Super Bowl game, will die in highway accidents this year. More than half of the accidents will involve alcohol.

are others. Psychologists would probably add certain characteristics of adolescence, such as the desire to experiment
with new situations or the tendency to be defiant and rebellious. Family turmoil and depression are also factors in
many cases.

Another reason is that young people are usually both
inexperienced drivers and inexperienced drinkers. Driving
demands the split-second calculation and skillful maneuver-
ing that come only from years behind the wheel. In addition,
alcohol, a central-nervous-system depressant, slows reaction
time and blurs judgment, further impairing the driver's ability
to handle the car.

Again and again research suggests that drunk driving is
not merely a traffic safety problem but a drinking problem,
as well. Young people have little guidance or supervision of
their drinking. They get the message from adults that drinking
is mature, but young people become intoxicated by smaller
amounts of alcohol than older people and more often drink
to get drunk rather than to relax and socialize. In many cases,
young people with drinking problems have a parent who
drinks heavily or is an alcoholic.

Tragically, many young people themselves are already
alcoholics. The National Institute of Alcohol Abuse estimates
that of the 6 million young drinkers nationwide, more than
half between the ages of 14 and 17 have problems with alcohol. There is also increasing evidence that the majority of
drunk drivers are alcoholics — seriously addicted to alcohol
— not just overindulging social drinkers, as law enforcement
officials once assumed.

Indeed, law enforcement, or the lack thereof, has played
a significant role in the widespread nature of the drunk-driving problem in the United States. Although drunk driving
plagues other developed countries as much as it does the
United States, the rest of the world has been quicker to pass
strict drunk-driving laws. In addition, although other countries may have higher traffic fatality rates, no other country
reports as high a rate of car ownership among young people
as does the United States. Also, Americans' admiration for
independence and individualism, coupled with the glorified
image of the "hard drivin', hard drinkin' " man, causes some
people to resist any kind of regulation of drinking and driving
habits.

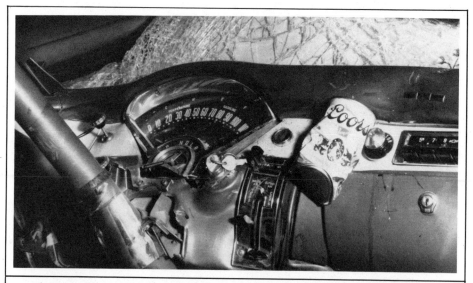

Alcohol slows down reaction time and blurs judgment, rendering the driver incapable of operating his vehicle safely. If alcohol is used in combination with other depressants, these effects are intensified.

Other Psychoactive Drugs

Other psychoactive drugs also impair driving. Marijuana is the third most frequently used drug in the United States, after alcohol and cigarettes, and has increased gradually in potency since the 1970s. Simulated driver tests have shown that marijuana — with its power to slow down reaction time and distort visual perceptions — dangerously interferes with the judgment and concentration that safe driving requires. Cocaine, the use of which has soared in the 1980s, induces feelings of false confidence that can lead to lethal recklessness behind the wheel. Amphetamines may temporarily increase alertness and endurance, but habitual use of these "pep pills" leads to distorted perceptions, and sometimes hallucinations, with obvious negative effects on driving skills. All sleeping pills, pain medications, and tranquilizers depress the central nervous system, leading to drowsiness, weakened concentration, and slower reflex actions. Even nonprescription over-the-counter drugs such as cough syrups and cold or allergy medications — with their tendency to induce drowsiness and lethargy — may have unexpected, disastrous effects on a driver. Moreover, the effects of psychoactive drugs are almost universally intensified when they are used in combination with alcohol.

What Can Be Done?

Are there solutions to the deadly problems that arise from mixing drugs, including alcohol, with driving? Fortunately, most states offer a wide variety of programs — drug-education programs, safe-rides programs, alcohol- and drug-free dances, proms, and graduation parties. Nationwide, the 1980s have witnessed a significant stiffening of penalties for DWI, and most states have raised the legal drinking age to 21. A few have even experimented with curfew hours. Still others have proposed prohibiting or restricting teenage driving.

Singly, however, none of these solutions addresses the drunk-driving problem in its totality. For example, a school drug-education program may heighten student awareness about the dangers of alcohol and other drugs, but it does little to change peer attitudes. A safe-rides program may save lives, but it does not address adolescent alcoholism. Laws are not effective if they are not enforced regularly. With this in mind, a complex combination of solutions seems necessary.

A book about drinking, driving, and drugs is not likely to change anyone's behavior. Bad habits and stressful environments are not remedied so easily. But a close examination of the problem shows that people can change — that anger and grief can be transformed into action and that "grass roots" organizations can make a difference. It reveals that a better understanding of our legal system and a better understanding of human behavior can form the basis of a multifaceted, effective assault on the havoc drugs cause on the highways.

Too many of our nation's young people have fallen prey to the deadly combination of drinking and driving. In order to change this sad fact, we must first try to understand the problem. Who are these young people? Why are they drinking? How and to what extent does drinking affect them? What are our laws doing to protect them as well as the rest of us? It is only after answering these questions that we may begin to find solutions. And it is only after finding those solutions that we may be able to stop the tragic toll of young lives lost every year.

Each community has its own tragic story to tell about the toll drunk driving has taken. The details are heartbreaking, and for those who are left behind, the experience is often shattering.

CHAPTER 1

WHO ARE THE VICTIMS?

Perhaps the accident happened five years ago. People may have forgotten the details. "There was drinking, for sure," someone remembers. "That's a dangerous bend at the bottom of that hill. Amazing that the tree is still alive. He was a nice kid. Drank too much, but a nice kid."

Or perhaps the accident was just last year, at graduation time. A senior and his date were speeding home to meet a curfew after the prom. The car, a new Chevrolet Camaro, a graduation present, careened out of control and crashed into a stone wall. The driver and passenger were crushed by the impact and killed instantly. Friends said the victims had "only" been drinking beer.

Nearly every community has stories like these to tell. The teens killed were drivers, passengers, or sometimes just innocent bystanders. There are heartbreaking details of dashed postgraduation ambitions and athletic promise. There is disbelief and a terrible sense of waste. This was the case in the story of Susan Herzog:

The party was at Gary's house, less than two miles from Susan's home in Fairfax, Virginia, a suburb of Washington, D.C. Gary, a classmate at Robinson Secondary School, was Susan's first serious boyfriend. Susan Herzog was what teachers call a "people person," vice-president of her senior class. A B student, Susan worked part-time doing phone surveys to save money for college — she hoped to major in early childhood education at Virginia Tech. She swam the breaststroke on the school swim team and had been picked by her principal for a panel on teenage alcohol abuse. Susan was not much of a drinker and when she and her friends went to parties, they carried six-packs of soft drinks.

Normally, Susan's weekend curfew was 1:00 A.M., but because it was New Year's Eve and her senior year, her parents had allowed her an extra half hour. Shortly after 1:00 she kissed Gary goodnight and headed home in the beloved blue Volkswagen bug her father had bought secondhand. She drove east on Commonwealth Boulevard, a gently curving road that glistened that night under a light rain. It was just after 1:15 when she headed up a slight hill less than a mile from her home.

Kevin Tunell, age 17, was feeling good after six or eight glasses of champagne. He boasted to his friends that he drove even better when he was drunk. As he headed home on the 30 miles-per-hour road the local kids call Commonwealth Mountain Speedway, his speedometer inched past 50.

At 1:18 A.M., Kevin's car crested a hill, crossed the double yellow line, hit Susan's VW head-on, and drove it back 20 yards onto someone's front lawn. Susan was killed instantly; her heart and every major organ in her body ruptured. Kevin had two bumps on his forehead and a scratch along the bridge of his nose.

Susan's story has received a lot of publicity. It has been told countless times by Kevin Tunell himself, who was sentenced not to a year in jail, as the Herzog family had hoped he would be, but to one year of giving speeches about his experience to teenage audiences. Kevin has told the story to church groups, schools, and colleges across the country, to magazine, radio, and television reporters, and even on "The Phil Donahue Show."

Recognizing the Victims

Susan Herzog had the terrible misfortune of being in the wrong place at the wrong time. She might have been a pedestrian, or a motorist changing a tire in a break-down lane. She might have been a child, a nursing mother, an elderly widow. She got in the way of a drunk driver, and she, instead of Kevin, paid the ultimate price. The death of the unsuspecting victim is perhaps the most senseless loss of all.

The second kind of victim is the passenger, sober or drunk, who rides with a drunk driver. Usually these passengers are friends who feel dependent on the driver for a ride home. Like their driver, they may be unable to judge how much they have had to drink or are simply too embarrassed to speak up. They are as likely to be female as male, as in the following example.

"At 1:18 A.M., Kevin's car crested a hill, crossed the double yellow line, hit Susan's VW head-on, and drove it back 20 yards onto someone's front lawn. Susan was killed instantly. . . ."

Anne was a lovely girl, with long dark hair and soft brown eyes. She was in her last year of high school and was looking forward to going to her senior prom, for which she had recently bought a white lace gown.

Just before Easter, Anne had a fight with her boyfriend, which left her depressed. Her friends took her out to a local restaurant to cheer her up, but while having dinner, she spotted her boyfriend's older brother, Fred, at the bar.

Leaving her friends, Anne sat with Fred while he drank, pouring out her troubles and asking his advice on what to do about his brother. Fred suggested that she come back to the house with him and make up with his brother that very night.

Anne hesitated, realizing that Fred had had a lot to drink. But the thought of making up with her boyfriend won out, so she grabbed her purse and followed Fred out to his black Corvette.

Less than half a mile from the restaurant, Fred's car raced over a hill at 70 miles per hour, crossed over the double yellow line, and crashed head-on into an oncoming Cadillac. Fred was killed instantly. Anne never regained consciousness and died one week later, on her 18th birthday. She was buried in her prom dress.

The third type of victim of teenage drunk driving harms or kills himself alone. Ignorant of or indifferent to the dangers of driving while under the influence of alcohol, many teenagers from all socioeconomic groups, and representing all levels of academic and athletic achievement have gotten behind the wheel of a car after having had too much to drink. Too often, the price they pay for this action is permanent injury or death. They may not take passengers or innocent bystanders with them, but the tragic toll in wasted promise is high nonetheless.

Recognizing the Offenders

Is it possible to identify those young people most likely to drive drunk or most likely to allow themselves to be the passengers of a drunk driver? Research and surveys continually point to a characteristic profile of such people, who

Drinking and Driving (Based on teenagers)								
November 1983– January 1984	Drinking alcoholic beverages	Smoking marijuana	Taking pills	Using cocaine	Using hard drugs	None of these	Don't drive	Number of interviews
NATIONAL	14%	7%	1%	*	*	65%	20%	416
SEX								
Young men	19	11	1	1	1	62	18	214
Young women	9	2	1	*	*	67	22	202
AGE								
13–15 years	2	1	*	*	*	67	30	219
16–18 years	24	12	1	1	1	62	10	196
REGION								
East	11	8	*	*	*	65	23	111
Midwest	19	4	*	*	*	66	28	141
South	17	5	*	1	*	66	15	107
West	6	10	4	2	2	62	24	57
URBANIZATION								
Central cities	17	9	2	1	1	62	16	125
Suburbs	12	6	*	*	*	62	23	152
Non-metropolitan	13	5	*	*	*	66	20	139
USE ALCOHOL	22	10	1	1	1	62	13	239
USE MARIJUANA	34	37	4	3	2	46	8	59
USE OTHER DRUGS	24	32	5	8	5	46	11	20

*Less than one percent.
NOTES: Totals exceed 100 percent due to multiple responses.
This survey was conducted on behalf of the COMPREHENSIVE CARE CORPORATION, INC.

unthinkingly put their own lives, the lives of their friends, and the lives of innocent strangers at risk. The chances of an alcohol-related accident are very high for certain individuals — their deaths are not just a random bad hand of cards. A 1983 *Weekly Reader* survey suggested that one out of every four students was "at risk" for involvement in an alcohol-related traffic accident at least once during the year.

Studies of adolescents involved in alcohol-related traffic accidents increasingly suggest a pattern: Young drunk drivers between the ages of 16 and 24 tend to be male, are frequent, heavy drinkers, are frequent drivers, and often do their drinking in cars. Those of high school age usually do average academic work. They may be involved in sports or social activities. Those beyond high school age often have prior traffic convictions and may be unemployed or have social and personal problems related to their drinking.

The following character — we will call him Bill — is an imaginary figure, a composite of many of the characteristics of young people who drink or use other drugs and drive.

Bill is a senior at a suburban high school, a good basketball player, and a fair student. He plans to attend a local university next year. His teachers seem to like him but sense that he is somewhat impulsive. His sense of humor has made him popular, and he manages to get invited to a party nearly every weekend. He just recently bought his first car, a secondhand Ford Corvair.

Bill started drinking occasionally when he was about 12 1/2, wanting to feel accepted by his 15-year-old brother and his friends. At weekend parties, Bill sometimes drinks — mostly beer — just to get drunk. He and his friends pride themselves on being able to "put away a six-pack." His father is a heavy drinker, and Bill senses that his parents accept his drinking, perhaps because they have said nothing more than just "Don't drink and drive."

After blacking out at a recent party and upsetting his new girlfriend, Bill has been trying to drink less. But he enjoys the feeling of confidence he has after drinking. He claims that he is more comfortable talking with girls when he is high.

He has tried amphetamines but stopped using them after a lecture given by his basketball coach, whom he admires, warned him off. Bill has smoked marijuana occasionally in a friend's car, once getting such a rush that he had to lie down in the backseat, his heart seeming to pound so hard he thought it would burst. He feels pressure occasionally to try other drugs but feels more comfortable sticking with beer; beer seems "safe."

Bill was driving illegally on back roads with his older brother almost as soon as his brother got his license. He breezed through driver-education class. He is confident and proud of his driving ability, though he has only had his license for two years.

Though some of this may sound familiar, most of us would exclude ourselves from any kind of "typical profile." We may think of ourselves as more responsible, having noth-

Passenger in Vehicle When Driver Was Under Influence (Based on teenagers)							
November 1983– January 1984	Alcoholic beverages	Marijuana	Pills	Cocaine	Hard drugs	None of these	Number of interviews
NATIONAL	36%	17%	5%	3%	1%	61%	416
SEX							
Young men	35	17	4	1	1	62	214
Young women	36	17	6	4	1	61	202
AGE							
13–15 years	17	6	2	2	1	81	219
16–18 years	54	27	8	4	1	42	196
REGION							
East	33	19	7	3	*	65	111
Midwest	39	15	4	1	2	59	141
South	34	16	4	1	*	59	107
West	37	18	4	8	2	63	57
URBANIZATION							
Central cities	38	28	7	4	1	59	125
Suburbs	32	11	3	3	*	58	152
Non-metropolitan	38	14	4	*	*	58	139
USE ALCOHOL	49	24	7	4	1	48	239
USE MARIJUANA	73	61	19	13	3	20	59
USE OTHER DRUGS	73	73	41	22	8	16	20

*Less than one percent
NOTES: Totals exceed 100 percent due to multiple responses.
This survey was conducted on behalf of the COMPREHENSIVE CARE CORPORATION, INC.

ing to do with the kind of crowd that drinks and uses other drugs. Unfortunately, however, statistics show that many adolescents routinely drink beer at parties. The chances that even nondrinking young people will find themselves in a car with a driver who has been drinking are actually quite strong. It can be terribly difficult for any passenger to say no to a good friend who happens to be less than sober. Faced with a curfew set by trusting, anxious parents, many young people risk death rather than call home for a ride.

The choices that confront drinking drivers and their passengers are faced by any number of young people from time to time: Should I take my chances and try to make it home on time, knowing that I myself or the driver has had too much to drink? Or should I just say no to any offer of a drink or a ride home from someone who's been drinking?

Car ownership can represent popularity, maturity, and freedom to a teenager, but recent research has linked it to lower school grades, increased traffic violations, drunk driving, and accidents.

CHAPTER 2

WHAT DRIVES THEM TO DRINK AND DRIVE?

It sounded like a simple exercise, perhaps even a little silly. A group of young people on a weekend drug prevention retreat were asked by their group leader to take turns saying no individually to each person in a circle. Just walk around the group, stop in front of each person, look each one in the eyes, and quietly, but firmly, say no.

The young people found the task surprisingly difficult. To reject their peers — even in a group exercise — seemed fundamentally unnatural. A few participants broke down in tears and could not make it through the exercise. For others the word "no" seemed to stick in their throats. Everyone expressed feelings of rejection, fear, and isolation. There was general relief when the exercise was over.

This scene was filmed for a nationally televised program called "Frontline." But that is not what makes it seem familiar. The feelings hit home — we can all empathize with the vulnerable expressions on the faces of the young people. Adults and young people have all "been there," have all felt the joy of being part of the "gang" and the terrible pain of being left

Adolescents hang out on the street late at night. There is often a temptation to abuse the freedom that comes with a driver's license, especially if one is encouraged by one's peers to act irresponsibly.

out. Our peer group of friends and acquaintances controls to a large extent how we feel about ourselves. Acceptance by peers can relieve feelings of insecurity and stress that can be especially strong during adolescence.

Peer pressure is a familiar and inescapable fact of life. Most often, the term has negative connotations. It suggests pressure to do something only to be part of the peer group, not necessarily because it feels natural or right. The hardest kind of peer pressure to resist is the subtle kind that builds up, that nags. You may make a decision with which you feel comfortable but experience daily pressure to change your mind. Without other peers to reinforce your decision, that kind of pressure is hard to resist.

In one survey after another, young people cite peer pressure as the primary reason they start drinking or using other drugs. A 1983 *Weekly Reader* survey of 100,000 fourth- to twelfth-graders showed "other kids" were the most important influence in "making drugs and drinking seem like fun." In answer to the question "How much do kids your age push each other to try beer, wine, liquor, or marijuana?" more than 75% of the students in grades 9–12 responded that they felt either "some" or "a lot" of pressure to try alcohol. More than 65% felt pressure to try marijuana. Younger students named peers as their source of information about drugs and drinking, much of it undoubtedly inaccurate.

Peer pressure probably has just as much to do with drug abuse and risk taking in other countries as it does in the United States. Among a group of young drivers in London, England, peer influence was a stronger motivating factor in decisions to drink and drive than any consideration of personal safety. Similarly, educators in Saskatchewan, Canada, also found their school-based drug-education program not nearly as influential as the students' home environment and peer group.

Peer pressure can also have a positive influence on teenagers. In the search for approval, pressure to abstain from using drugs can play a large part in a decision to resist such experimentation.

Putting Peer Pressure to Work

Fortunately, peer pressure works in two ways and can be a positive influence as well as a negative one. The same desire for approval that leads one person to experiment with drugs can help another person resist such experimentation. It all depends on whom you are trying to please. For example, in a 1980 study of the impact of drunk-driving penalties, young drivers ranked the reasons they would not drink and drive in the following order:

1. peer disapproval

2. moral commitment to laws

3. risk of lawbreaking—fear of penalties

4. parental disapproval

Peer disapproval is an especially strong deterrent for girls. Boys report they do not want to suffer legal penalties for drunk driving but feel that disappointing friends is a likelier consequence than being arrested. Interestingly, the risk of suffering an accident and death was not even listed as a deterrent in this study.

The most successful alcohol- and drug-prevention programs are those that use positive peer reinforcement. Some programs train young people to lead discussion groups. Older students may teach younger students. When a group of trained senior-high students walks into a junior-high classroom, the younger students sit up and take notice. They may be more likely to accept what the high school students have to say about drugs than to believe a teacher.

Beyond Peer Pressure

But peer pressure is not the only motivating force behind teenagers taking that first drink and getting behind the wheel of a car. In fact, adolescents turn to alcohol for a combination of reasons ranging from a simple, if misguided, urge to have fun to a perhaps unconscious effort to "medicate" themselves for serious emotional distress.

Some adolescents are unable to deal responsibly with the freedom that comes with their driver's license. Learning to drive and getting a license can be a very positive experi-

IS IT WORTH THE PRICE ?

Being arrested for drunk driving is very expensive. After adding attorney fees and the increased cost of auto insurance after a drunk driving arrest, Marion High School students figured it would cost them a minimum of $3,200 to be arrested.

Here is a list of what students can buy with $3,200.

One year of college	400 albums or tapes	80 pairs of shoes	2,660 gal. of gas	119 pairs of jeans
Two-fifths of a new car	9,143 candy bars	2,286 fast-food hamburgers	12,800 arcade video games	914 movies	246 concerts	2,133 school activities
3,555½ school lunches	6,400 doughnuts	64 ski trips ($50 per trip)	17.8 portable stereos	6,400 soft drinks	324.9 pizzas	376½ haircuts

Being arrested for drunk driving is an expensive proposition. Legal fees and increased insurance costs can amount to thousands of dollars.

ence for many teens. But pressure to have a license by age 16 or 17 can be harmful if the teen is not ready to deal with the attendant responsibilities. By the same token, actually owning a car, however much adolescents may long to do so, carries with it a set of obligations that many young people cannot meet. Although car ownership represents popularity, independence, and maturity, research shows that it heightens the risk of an accident. One study associated car ownership with lower school grades, speeding, drunk driving, and traffic violations — all in addition to accidents. Too often, teenagers are unable to view driving as a privilege and a responsibility, and too often, many teenagers pay for this mistake with their lives.

Apart from the complications that can arise from car ownership, another contributing factor that can aggravate or precipitate drinking and driving is a troubled personal life.

Family problems and tension at home can cause many teenagers to become depressed and rebellious, making them increasingly susceptible to the pitfalls of substance abuse, including driving while intoxicated.

Family problems or tension at home, for instance, can have a negative effect on teenagers. Many become alienated from their parents and end up depressed, resentful, or rebellious — and increasingly susceptible to the pitfall of drinking and driving. Many parents ignore the signals, thus appearing to condone the reckless behavior, which can escalate and, if continued unchecked, end tragically.

On a more positive note, parental attitudes toward drugs can have enormous positive influence, especially if established when their children are still young. Parents can encourage communication on all subjects with their children, who will then feel that their questions are welcomed. They can make a point of being well-informed about drugs. Above all, parents must show moderation in their own drug use. Too often, parents suffer from the same misinformation or ambivalence as their children do.

Parents who are rigid about abstaining from all drugs, however, or who feel uncomfortable discussing drugs may foster rebelliousness in their offspring, who are then forced to go outside the home to find any information. Also, parents who are heavy drinkers or alcoholics set an example of irresponsible drinking and, sometimes, driving that their children later struggle to resist, often unsuccessfully.

There is also recent evidence to suggest that driving while under the influence is more prevalent in small towns than it is in cities and more common among boys than among girls. In a study of licensed teenage drivers in rural towns, 25% of the boys said they had driven after drinking, compared with 11% of the girls. In one rural community, 40% of the students in grades 10–12 said they had driven after 2 drinks. Among 75 young people arrested for various traffic violations, 68% reported illegal alcohol and drug use, and 31% reported having consumed 4 or more different kinds of drugs prior to their arrest.

Whatever the cause — peer pressure, increased responsibility, feelings of alienation from parents — once a teenager takes that first drink at a party, aware that he is driving home that night, he is risking not only his life but the lives of his passengers, fellow motorists, and pedestrians. For although he may brag that he can throw back a few beers and still drive competently, maybe even better than when completely sober, the truth is that already the drug is affecting his body in significant ways of which he is unaware and over which he has no control.

A policeman helps members of the student organization BACCHUS stage a drinking and driving demonstration. The experiment proved that just two drinks can seriously impair driving performance.

CHAPTER 3

THE BODY'S RESPONSE

How much alcohol can the average individual consume before driving performance is impaired? A group of students belonging to an organization called "BACCHUS" (Blood Alcohol Consciousness Concerning Health of University Students) at the University of Kentucky wanted to find out. They arranged a drinking-and-driving demonstration, laying out a driving course with traffic cones in a parking lot. They asked well-known campus leaders to drink a measured amount of alcohol and attempt to drive the course. At half-hour intervals the drivers had to drink another measure of alcohol. As the drivers became intoxicated, they grew careless and boastful about their poor performances. Within two hours, several traffic cones, each representing a pedestrian, had been knocked over.

The driving performance of most people deteriorates after they consume relatively little alcohol. Two drinks, each containing three-fourths of an ounce of alcohol, are enough to increase reaction time and decrease muscle coordination. A small person drinking on an empty stomach may be adversely affected by just one drink. Teenagers typically arc affected by alcohol more quickly than are adults. In older heavy drinkers impairment may not seem as obvious or as rapid.

Sue is 15 and weighs 106 pounds. She arrives at Bob's party at 10 P.M. and takes the first beer that is offered to her. It is her first drink of the evening.

At about 10:20 P.M., she goes to get her second beer. On her way across the room to the cooler, she feels slightly dizzy and unsteady but blames it on not having eaten much.

Halfway through her second beer, Sue begins to feel funny. She is unable to fully concentrate on conversations. Seeing Matt, a boy she has a crush on, she saunters over to talk to him. Before now, Sue had been too shy to approach Matt. Suddenly, however, she finds herself chatting with him, and even asking him to dance.

Thrilled with her newfound confidence, Sue accepts Matt's offer to get her another beer. Matt returns with her drink and they begin talking again. Soon, however, Sue notices that her tongue feels thick and that she is stumbling over her words. Matt has begun to look blurry, and her head is beginning to spin.

When Matt asks her to dance again she accepts, but finds herself unable to coordinate her arm and leg movements. Her balance seems off and every-thing is spinning.

Explaining how she feels to Matt, Sue is re-lieved when he offers to find her a cup of coffee. Coffee, he assures her, is a surefire method for sob-ering up.

After she has finished her coffee, Sue discovers that Matt is right — she does feel much better. She believes that she is completely sober now and ready to drive home . . .

Because alcohol is already a liquid, the body can absorb it remarkably fast. It is highly fat- and water-soluble. About 20% goes directly into the bloodstream from the stomach. The rest enters the body from the small intestine. Just mo-ments after alcohol enters the bloodstream, it reaches the cerebral cortex, the area of the brain responsible for judg-ment, self-control, and reason. There alcohol acts as a de-pressant, slowing down all mental processes. Because the areas of the brain governing caution and self-control are among the first to be affected, most people feel more relaxed

Because of their lighter body weight and their relative inexperience with alcohol, teenagers tend to become intoxicated faster and more visibly than adults.

and uninhibited after just one or two drinks. After three or four drinks, speech, vision, coordination, and balance are increasingly impaired.

Once alcohol is absorbed, the body burns it off at a constant, slow rate. Nothing but time can change the rate at which a person becomes sober again. Cold showers do not help. Neither does coffee, though it may seem to give a momentary lift. Some high-protein foods such as milk, eggs, and cheese can help delay the absorption of alcohol, but only if they are eaten immediately before or while drinking. A quick succession of strong drinks (10–40% alcohol) on an empty stomach spells the greatest danger, with their effects lasting for hours.

Blood Alcohol Concentration

One of the terms mentioned in any discussion of drinking and driving is blood alcohol concentration (BAC). Blood alcohol levels are given in milligrams of alcohol per 100 milliliters of blood. A reading of 50 mg. of alcohol per 100 ml. of blood would be written as a blood alcohol content (BAC) of .05. That is the equivalent of about two drinks consumed during a two-hour period. After four drinks consumed during a two-hour period, the BAC usually exceeds .10, the point of legal intoxication in most states in the United States. According to Canadian and British traffic laws, driving with any BAC above .08 is illegal. In Scandinavia and the Netherlands the legal limit at which one can drink and drive is still lower —.05.

There is nothing magical about the illegal .10 BAC designation. Some people are incapable of driving safely at much lower blood alcohol levels, while a small percentage seem in control at .10 BAC. Some of the difference has to do with body weight. Generally, an individual weighing 160 pounds would be over the legal limit after consuming a six-pack of beer within two hours. But based on alcohol's effects on the average person, the chances of an accident double at a BAC of .06. At .10 BAC, they are 6 times greater, and at .15 BAC they are 25 times greater.

One can of beer (12 to 16 ounces of 4 1/2% alcohol) can raise a drinker's BAC just as much as a glass of wine or

A truck driver being arrested for DWI. People are considered legally drunk in most states when their BAC reaches .10. However, many people are incompetent to drive long before they reach this point.

as a cocktail containing 1 1/2 ounces of "hard liquor" such as whiskey. An ounce of beer does not contain as much alcohol as an ounce of whiskey, but beer is usually served in much larger portions than other drinks. The mind-altering chemical component in alcohol, called ethanol, is exactly the same in beer as in any other alcoholic drink. The same thing is true of rum, vodka, gin, whiskey, or bourbon: Distilled liquors with the same "proof" are equally intoxicating. Proof refers to alcohol content; 80 proof means about 40% alcohol.

Stimulants and Driving

If a depressant drug like alcohol slows down the brain, what about drugs that are stimulants, such as amphetamines or cocaine? Would they speed up and improve driving performance?

Speed up? — yes, dangerously! Improve? — no. Amphetamines can suppress appetite and increase wakefulness. They are often used by truck drivers, airplane pilots, and soldiers in a misguided attempt to stay awake for long stretches of time. Students sometimes take stimulants to cram all night for exams. But while amphetamines may help hold off sleep, there is a trade-off in mental performance. Amphetamines do produce wakefulness, but they cannot eliminate fatigue. In turn, the fatigued mind cannot solve problems well or focus attention for very long. Drivers who take amphetamines tend to experience an exaggerated sense of self-confidence and are more likely to take risks. For example, there are numerous cases of people under the influence of amphetamines being hit by trains while driving an automobile because they were convinced that they could beat the train.

Like amphetamines, cocaine can impair judgment and persuade a young person to drive fast, beyond his or her control. A young, unlicensed driver may feel fearless behind the wheel. These exhilarating feelings can continue for 45 minutes to 2 hours, usually followed by depression and fatigue. Users then usually want to take more of the drug to ward off the resulting depression. Large doses of cocaine can cause hallucinations, panic reactions, and abrupt changes in perception. Studies also show that accidents are more likely to happen to individuals under the influence of cocaine.

The Sedative Drugs

Barbiturates and tranquilizers, the sedative drugs, are as dangerous as stimulants. The first stages of sedative intoxication are similar to alcohol intoxication. Typically, there is a decrease in feelings of social inhibition and increased relaxation. In later stages, sluggishness and lack of motor coordination are evident, both of which can obviously be detrimental to driving ability.

Marijuana creates special hazards for drivers. Some tests show that marijuana causes just as many errors in driving performance as alcohol. Marijuana increases reaction time, and for a driver, a delay in braking time can be fatal. Marijuana also may accentuate light glare, temporarily blinding a night driver facing oncoming headlights. Laboratory tests show that the drug alters other visual and time perceptions, causes difficulties in concentration, and distorts hearing. Any of the temporary physical effects of marijuana, such as rapid heartbeat or throat irritation, can be distracting. Inexperienced marijuana users generally experience these effects more forcefully than do experienced users, but the danger exists in both cases. A hallucinogen, marijuana's effects are highly dependent upon the amount of tetrahydrocannabinol (THC), the psychoactive chemical, contained in each dose. A "joint" of low potency (1% THC) might pose little danger to a driver. However, most marijuana currently on the illegal drug market is far stronger than that, containing 5 to 20% THC. Because potency varies, even experienced users may be surprised by the powerful physical effects of the drug.

On the whole, marijuana users have a greater than average number of tickets for driving violations and are involved in a greater than average number of accidents. Furthermore, when marijuana is used in combination with alcohol, as it so often is by teenagers, who underestimate both drugs, the statistics for violations and accidents become much worse.

Over-the-Counter Drugs

What about nonprescription over-the-counter drugs such as allergy medications, antacids, sleeping pills, painkillers, and cold remedies? It has been estimated that 30 different drugs can be found in the average American household, 24 of them

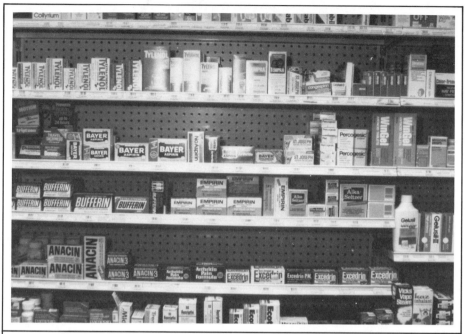

Many people consider nonprescription drugs harmless, but some of these substances contain chemicals that can cause drowsiness and dizziness. Such preparations should not be taken prior to driving.

nonprescription. Many of these drugs carry a warning label that reads: "Caution: Avoid driving a motor vehicle or operating heavy machinery. Avoid alcoholic beverages while taking this product." The danger in all these drugs is that many people consider any drug available without a prescription harmless. Believing that if a little cold medication is helpful, a lot can do wonders, such people overmedicate themselves.

Nonprescription drugs are used so casually in our culture that people tend to forget how many different kinds of seemingly "harmless" drugs they may have ingested in the course of a day. After a few drinks in the evening, they may feel dizzy or even black out and never guess that the decongestant capsules they took earlier in the day were responsible.

Though any and all drugs can have unpleasant side effects and adversely affect driving, they are many times more dangerous when combined with alcohol. Alcohol tends to mul-

Times Driven a Car When Had Too Much to Drink						
	Never	Once	A few times	Many times	Don't know/ No answer	Number of interviews
Total	59%	10%	23%	7%	1%	(506)
Sex						
Male	51	10	29	9	1	(272)
Female	68	9	16	6	1	(233)
Frequency of drinking						
2–3 times a week or more	33	10	42	14	1	(132)
2–3 times a month/once a week	48	19	29	3	1	(150)
Once a month or less	77	6	14	3	*	(73)
Friends with drinking problem						
Yes	42	8	30	18	2	(121)
No	65	10	20	4	1	(384)
Plan to cut down/quit drinking						
Yes	25	21	44	10	*	(55)
No	52	11	29	7	1	(299)

*Less than one percent.

tiply the effects of other drugs, increasing the chances of severe reactions and overdose. For example, alcohol and cocaine in combination will produce both intoxication and euphoria. The sense of well-being may mask the intoxication and deceive a driver into feeling fully in control. The driver may ordinarily be sensible enough to ask for a ride home, but the cocaine may persuade him to throw caution to the wind.

Depressant drugs such as barbiturates are especially dangerous when taken by a person who has already had a lot to drink. Because alcohol and barbiturates are both depressants, when used in combination, they can slow down vital cell action so much as to be fatal.

In party settings, more than one drug is often available. This is especially true at teenage drinking parties. After a few drinks, the temptation to experiment with a new drug is harder to resist. Not surprisingly, most young people who are heavy drinkers also use other psychoactive drugs.

Ironically, some parents express relief if they hear a son or daughter has gotten into trouble with alcohol — relief that the trouble was not caused by other illegal, presumably more dangerous drugs. They forget that alcohol is illegal in most states for those under the age of 21 and that when alcohol is present at teenage parties, other illegal drugs are likely to be on hand as well. In most driving accidents involving psychoactive drugs other than alcohol, the drugs were used in combination with alcohol.

Few drugs are more dangerous than alcohol, though it is socially accepted in almost all cultures. Not only is heavy drinking at parties unhealthy in itself, but it is often a warning sign that pervasive problems with alcohol are in the making.

Police estimate that they pick up only about one in 2,000 drunk drivers. Of those they do pick up, it is thought that close to 80% are problem drinkers or alcoholics.

CHAPTER 4

ALCOHOLISM

By the time that most drunk drivers are finally arrested, they have generally been in trouble with alcohol for quite some time. There have been countless drinking bouts and many other occasions when they have been drunk behind the wheel. They may have been arrested before for disorderly conduct, assault and battery, or other alcohol-related crimes. They may have difficulty holding down a job, problems at school, or conflicts at home. DWI is a serious charge, but it can be a symptom of a more serious underlying problem — alcoholism.

Evidence increasingly suggests that many drunk drivers are alcoholics, not just the social drinkers they were once believed to be. In Quincy, Massachusetts, a district court studied 1,252 people convicted of drunken driving to assess their drinking habits. They found that 82% were problem drinkers; only 18% were social drinkers. In Pennsylvania a similar study revealed a total of 78% problem drinkers and 22% social drinkers. However, some police experts disagree with these figures, saying that it is too difficult to distinguish between a heavy drinker and an alcoholic. They believe that most drinkers simply misjudge their capacity for alcohol and have the poor sense to drive drunk and the bad luck to be arrested.

If that is the case, these drivers have extremely bad luck, for police estimate that they pick up only one in 2,000 drunk drivers. Odds that low suggest that those who do get caught probably drive drunk habitually. In addition, the average BAC among those arrested for drunk driving is .18 to .20, levels far higher than anyone but an alcoholic could tolerate.

What Is Alcoholism?

Alcoholism is an addiction to alcohol, similar in some ways to other drug addictions. Alcoholism is a disease; the alcoholic does not drink because he wants to but because he feels his body has to have the next drink. Initially, drinking makes the alcoholic feel better, but over time it actually makes him feel worse.

Though there are some accounts of "instant addiction," most alcoholics seem to start off as social or party drinkers who gradually find that they must drink increasingly larger

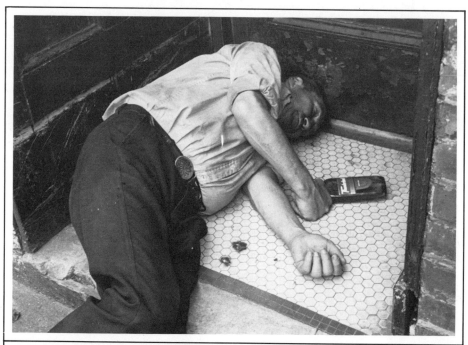

Alcoholics have been stereotyped as ne'er-do-wells and down-and-outers. In fact, this disease afflicts people from all walks of life.

Most alcoholics start out as social drinkers. As their illness advances, they must drink more and more to achieve the same effect.

amounts of alcohol to get high and who drink only to get high. For most adults, the decline from social drinker to alcoholic takes about five years.

What is the difference between problem drinking and alcoholism? Most experts agree that they are one and the same. Alcoholism has recognizable, progressive stages, and any of the early stages might be called problem drinking. Basically, uncontrolled drinking creates a host of problems, some of which the drinker may think he can solve by drinking more. Not the least of those problems is drunk driving. The alcoholic driver does not make a rational decision to drive, just as he does not make a rational decision to have the next drink. Both his drinking and his driving have gone beyond his control.

As an illness, alcoholism cuts across lines of social class, race, religion, age, and sex. It has been compared to heart disease or cigarette addiction in that anyone can succumb to it. Certain groups of people, such as children of alcoholics, seem to have a higher risk of developing alcoholism, but this may just as likely be caused by learned behavior as by physical intolerance to alcohol. The poor "Skid Row" bum is not the typical alcoholic but the product of myths and prejudice. In one poll, 21–33% of Americans say that alcohol abuse has brought problems to their families. An alcoholic is as likely to be a businesswoman, an electrician, a doctor, a teacher, or a high school student as a stereotypical down-and-outer.

Although most people consider alcoholism an adult problem, it is estimated that more than half of the nation's 6 million young drinkers have problems with alcohol. Teenagers urge one another to drink. They often drink to get drunk, not to be social. In teenagers, the progression from social drinking to alcoholism is much faster than in adults, taking just one year instead of five. In young people, alcoholism exacts heavier penalties, stunting emotional and academic growth, lowering resistance to infection, and impairing reflexes. Moreover, alcoholism is often not diagnosed in teenagers until after the illness has done substantial damage.

Getting Help

Once alcoholism is diagnosed, however, teenagers stand a good chance of recovery. Alcoholism can be cured. Alcoholics recover in the same way cigarette smokers recover: They stop. This "cure" for alcoholism is taken one day at a time for the rest of the alcoholic's life. It usually requires support and reinforcement from other recovered alcoholics and the alcoholic's friends and family. No alcoholic ever recovered by simply getting arrested for drunk driving and having his license taken away. No conventional classes on responsible drinking can alone bring about sobriety. The most sensible way alcoholics recover is by finding a program that recognizes their special needs.

Alcoholics Anonymous (AA) is the best-known and most successful program available to help the alcoholic. AA describes itself as a fellowship of men and women who help each other to stay sober. The only requirement for membership in AA is a desire to stop drinking. AA members achieve this not by swearing off drinking forever but by deciding not to drink for 24 hours — concentrating not on the future but on today.

Members admit that they are never cured but become "recovered" alcoholics. For recovered alcoholics, "one drink is too many, and a thousand are not enough." For many AA members, the road back to sobriety is a powerful spiritual experience, accomplished with the understanding and support of other AA members.

AA meetings are held seven days a week, during both the day and evening, in churches, clubhouses, and other meeting halls throughout the United States and much of the rest of the world. At first, these meetings may seem like any social gathering. A few people mill about drinking coffee, chatting, and laughing quietly. Most people in the room are listening to a young woman tell about her anxiety at school during the past week or to an older man describe how he felt like an outsider when he first visited the group. One by one, members stand up and talk about their drinking, express

It is estimated that more than half of the 6 million adolescent drinkers in the United States have a problem with alcohol. As a group, teenagers are more likely than adults to drink just to get drunk.

Are You in Trouble with Alcohol?

1. Do you lose time from school as a result of drinking?

2. Do you drink because you are shy with other people?

3. Do you drink to build up your self-confidence?

4. Do you drink alone?

5. Is drinking affecting your reputation — or do you care?

6. Do you drink to escape from study or home worries?

7. Do you feel guilty or "bummed out" after drinking?

8. Does it bother you if someone says that maybe you drink too much?

9. Do you have to take a drink when you go out on a date?

10. Do you make-out (in general) better when you drink?

11. Do you get into financial troubles over buying liquor?

12. Do you feel a sense of power when you drink?

13. Have you started hanging out with a crowd where booze is easy to get?

14. Have you lost friends since you've started drinking?

15. Do your friends drink LESS than you do?

16. Do you drink until the bottle is empty?

17. Have you ever had a complete loss of memory from drinking?

18. Have you ever been to a hospital or been busted due to drunk driving?

19. Do you "turn off" any studies or lectures about drinking?

20. Do you THINK you have a problem with alcohol?

One YES indicates danger, two a high probability, and three a clear problem.

their current needs, or explain how the program has helped them. Each speaker begins by saying:

Hi. My name is _____(first name only). I am an alcoholic. Or:
Hi. My name is _____. I am an alcoholic and an addict.

Some people choose to remain silent and listen. If this is an "open meeting," there may be friends or family members present. "Closed meetings" are for alcoholics only.

Al-Anon and Alateen are similar self-help groups, designed for adults and adolescents, respectively, who are trying to come to terms with the alcoholism of a spouse, parent, or other loved one. As is the case with AA, there are no fees or dues, and participation is anonymous. People may attend and simply listen. Many members are the children of alcoholics who, before they sought group support, felt frightened and isolated and may have become alcoholics themselves.

An estimated 28.6 million Americans, or one out of every eight people, are the children of alcoholics. The National Association for Children of Alcoholics now holds annual conventions and helps members regain a positive sense of self-worth. In Somerville, Massachusetts, a program called CASPAR (Cambridge and Somerville Program for Alcoholism Rehabilitation) gives special attention to the children of alcoholics. In peer-led discussion groups, the young people learn how to cope with conflicts at home and develop healthier, more responsible attitudes about drinking.

As concern about teenage drinking grows, hospitals across the country have started special programs to help young people and their families. But this will solve only part of the drinking and driving problem. Stringent law enforcement is also a necessary part of the plan to combat drunk driving.

Fighting Back

Many organizations, companies, schools, and individuals have pitched in to fight the tragic annual loss of thousands of lives to drinking and driving. Nationwide, TV and radio commercials broadcast their plea: Don't Drink and Drive. Magazine ads graphically depict the frequently fatal consequences of drunk driving.

More often than not, teenagers are the victims of alcohol-related accidents, and special campaigns have been created to speak directly to them. As part of this effort, the Reader's Digest Foundation challenged U.S. advertising agencies to create hard-hitting anti-drunk-driving posters. The winning posters were then sent out to selected high schools to be used as part of programs against drunk driving. Here is a sampling of these posters.

NOT EVERYONE WHO DRIVES DRUNK DIES.

Before you drive drunk or get into a car with someone who's been drinking, remember this. You could live to regret it.

You have the right to drink.
You have the right to drive.

You have the right to remain silent.

Don't drink and drive.
Don't ride with anyone who does.

THERE ARE NO HEROES IN THIS LOCKER ROOM.

Please Don't Drink and Drive.

This is no place for a class reunion.

Last year, 15,000 teenagers were killed
in alcohol-related traffic accidents.
If you've been drinking, don't drive.
And if you see your friends drinking,
tell them not to drive.

You don't have to be drunk to be hurt by drunk driving.

ONE FOR THE ROAD.

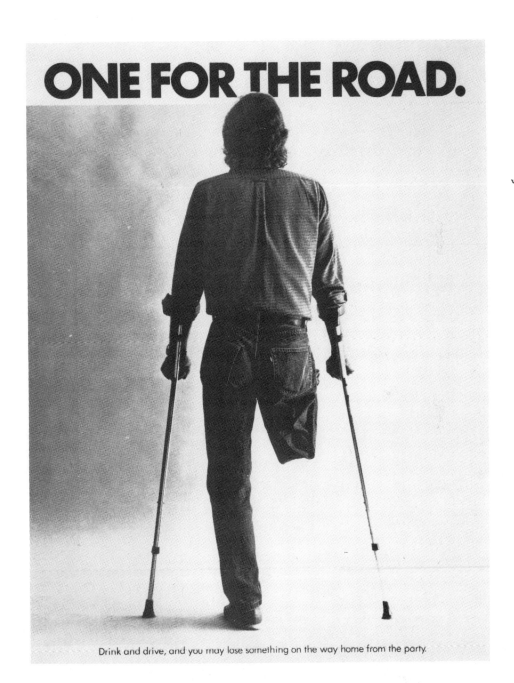

Drink and drive, and you may lose something on the way home from the party.

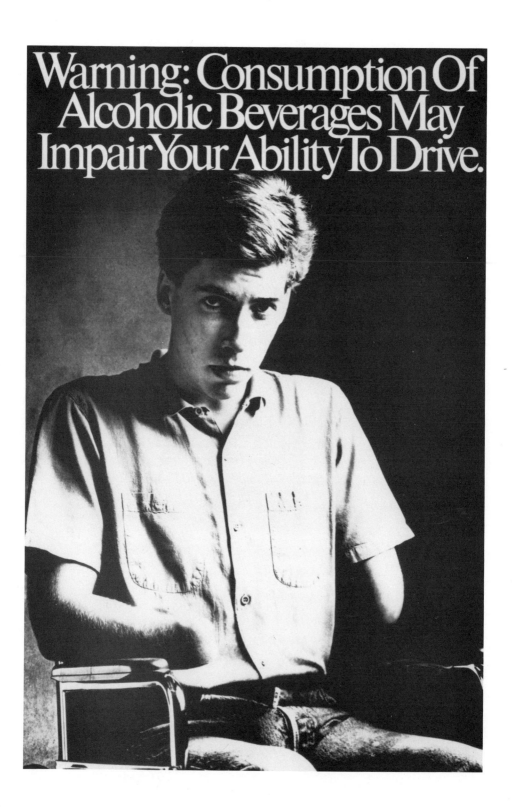

Most of the damage caused by drunk driving can easily be fixed in a body shop.

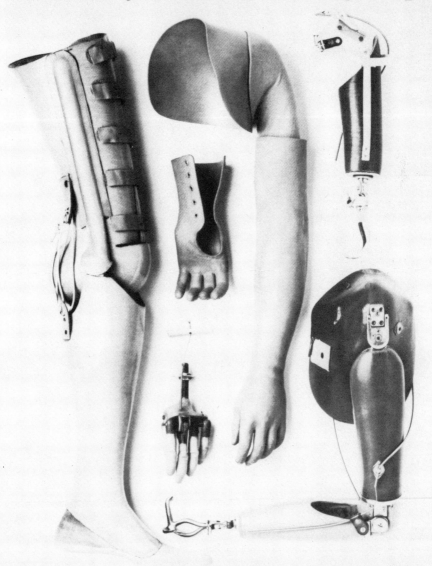

Don't drive drunk.
Dying isn't the only thing that could happen to you.

In 1982, these college students protested New Jersey's decision to raise the legal drinking age from 19 to 21. Although there are reasonable arguments for allowing those under 21 legal access to alcohol, statistics prove that raising the drinking age saves lives.

CHAPTER 5

IT'S AGAINST THE LAW

The minimum drinking age in most states is now 21. For people below that age, alcohol is as illegal as marijuana, cocaine, heroin, and other psychoactive drugs. Discussions about peer pressure and making choices, about DWI and BACs, become secondary in the face of this simple fact: Drinking by teenagers is against the law.

But it was not always so. During the Vietnam War era, 18-year-olds were given the right to vote; 18-, 19-, and 20-year-olds were fighting and dying for their country. At that time, all but two states had a minimum drinking age of 21. To most people it did not make sense to deny those young people the adult privilege of drinking. By the mid-1970s, most states had lowered their legal drinking age to 18.

Then the slaughter on the highways escalated. Injuries and deaths involving young drivers doubled and tripled: by 54% in Michigan, for example, and by 100% in Massachusetts. The most significant increase came from nighttime accidents involving single vehicles driven by 18- to 20-year-old males — accidents that nearly always involved alcohol. Alarmed by this tragic turn of events, legislators began to reverse the trend. Most favored a consistent, federally regulated drinking age; too many young people had been buying alcohol in

NOTICE

YOU MUST BE **21** TO BE SERVED

Section 65, Subdivision 1 of the New York State Alcoholic Beverage Control Law states:

"No person shall sell, deliver or give away or cause or permit or procure to be sold, delivered or given away any alcoholic beverages to any person, actually or apparently, under the age of twenty-one years." (Effective December 1, 1985)

New York State Liquor Authority

Notices such as this one are posted by law in bars across the country. By the middle of 1987, 37 states had raised the drinking age to 21.

neighboring states with a lower drinking age and then dying in accidents on the drive home. In 1984, the Reagan administration passed the "21" law, which penalized states with a drinking age under 21 by withholding 5% of their federal highway funds. By the middle of 1987, 37 states had raised the drinking age to 21.

The 21-year-old drinking age is still controversial. There are many reasonable, articulate arguments for allowing people younger than 21 legal access to alcohol. Some people say the law cannot be enforced or that alcohol becomes more enticing when it is illegal. Some states have tried to compromise, allowing 18-year-olds only wine or beer, apparently unaware that beer is the most common beverage involved in alcohol-related crashes.

But the bottom line is that raising the drinking age saves lives. In 1975, 8,996 drivers ages 18 to 20 died. In 1984, 7,797 died — 1,199 fewer deaths. The 18-year-old population was somewhat smaller in 1984 than a decade before, but at least 30% of the reduction in fatalities has been attributed to raising the drinking age. Unfortunately, fatalities among 16-

and 17-year-olds are not affected by changing the drinking age, suggesting that younger drinkers continue to obtain alcohol regardless of the law.

Drunk-driving legislation in this century has depended in part on how much scientists and politicians have understood about the drunk-driving problem. In the 1920s and 1930s, DWI was already a concern, but there were no reliable ways to measure exactly how much alcohol caused the problem. Many people felt sympathy for drunk drivers, believing that they were moderate drinkers, much like themselves, who happened to overindulge on one occasion. Juries tended to impose lenient sentences. But in the 1940s and 1950s measurement devices became more precise. By the early 1960s scientists were able to designate a blood alcohol level of .10

A newspaper cartoon satirizes the sort of attorney who helps offenders beat drunk driving charges. In general, however, the legal community supports more stringent anti–drunk driving laws.

as the limit beyond which most fatal accidents occurred. In 1966, a federal standard of .10 BAC for intoxication was established, and states were urged to adopt it. By 1981 every state had followed that advice. In 1985, the American Medical Association urged all states to set the legal limit much lower —at .05 BAC.

Today, any driver with a BAC of .10 or above can be arrested for DWI. Nearly every state has set up weekend roadblocks, called "sobriety checkpoints," to help enforce the law. Most states require the driver to take a preliminary breath test on a breath-analysis machine. The modern breath-analysis machine (sometimes called a "breathalyzer") is a solid-state, infrared breath-testing device that police claim is reliable to within 5/1000 of 1%. It is entirely automatic and cannot be tampered with by a police officer. Recent models can screen out substances that might produce false-positive readings. Some machines print out results on a multicopy ticket, one copy of which is given to the driver. A person who takes a breath test is entitled to an independent blood test, at his or her own expense.

Modern breath-analysis machines can measure only alcohol, not other drugs. Police who suspect a driver of being intoxicated on other drugs must search his or her person or car. A first offense for possession of three or more ounces of marijuana may bring a jail sentence of three to five years, though penalties vary from state to state.

Getting Tough

During the 1980s, rising concern about drunk driving led to a flood of new legislation. In 1982 alone, 378 bills relating to drunk driving were introduced in 37 states; 38 of these bills became the law in 25 states. About half of the states have mandatory seat-belt laws. Some states have open-container laws that prohibit any unsealed alcoholic beverage containers in the passenger compartment. Nearly all states have some kind of in-service DWI education for police officers and judges.

Much of the new legislation is aimed at bars, clubs, and restaurants. Most laws prohibit bars from serving obviously intoxicated customers. There are "killer bar" statutes that allow judges to ask defendants where they had their last drink.

The breath-analysis machine is a solid-state, infrared testing device that the police claim is reliable to within 5/1000 of 1%.

They then issue warnings to and exact stiff fines from those bars that do not refuse service to inebriated customers. Some states prohibit bars from holding evening "happy hours," when drinks are served at discount prices. "Happy hour" laws may prohibit serving one person more than two drinks at a time. Lawsuits for millions of dollars have been filed and won against bars serving drunk customers who have subsequently caused fatal accidents. As a result of legal suits, liquor liability insurance costs have skyrocketed, putting some bars and even some insurance companies out of business.

The changes in drunk-driving laws have made many barroom owners aware of their legal responsibility to keep drivers safe and sober. They know too well the crippling legal consequences they may suffer if one of their patrons causes an accident. The National Restaurant Association has sponsored designated-driver programs such as "I've Got the Key" or "Know When to Say When," engaging the attention of

Nearly every U.S. state has set up weekend roadblocks or sobriety checkpoints that help enforce drinking and driving laws.

restaurants, the media, and the community. Participating bars serve nonalcoholic beverages to the designated driver free of charge. "Know Your Limit" charts are posted in restrooms to help customers judge their sobriety by correlating body weight with number of drinks. A few bars have installed breathalyzers so that patrons can check their BAC themselves. Some bars have established a five-drink maximum or no longer serve especially potent drinks. Bartenders reinforce the message by wearing buttons that read: "Responsible drivers don't drive drunk" or "Don't drive after .05." There are special training programs for bartenders that teach them to recognize the telltale signs of inebriation.

In addition, several bars have joined together with towing companies to provide bar customers in out of the way regions with a safe ride home. The bartenders post signs offering this service, and customers are encouraged to come forward and admit that they need a ride home. For little more than car fare, towing companies will deliver the drinker to his front door. For a slightly higher fee, they will also tow his car. This system has met with considerable success in sparsely populated areas where taxis are never found and often, if the drinker wishes to return home, he must attempt to drive himself.

But many bars still make no effort to control their patrons' drinking. Some even flaunt such signs as "Marguarita Madness: $1.99 all week," encouraging binge drinking. In Massachusetts, a program called "Operation Last Call" was put into effect to monitor problem bars. Under "Operation Last Call" undercover officers mix with barroom customers. Customers who seem intoxicated are asked to submit to a breath-analysis test, and those who exceed the legal limit are taken into protective custody. In this way, drivers are stopped from becoming a public hazard before they get into their automobiles.

A few states also have a "social host liability law" under which a host or hostess in a private home can be sued if someone leaves the party intoxicated and causes an accident. Major distillers also risk being sued.

Despite host liability laws in effect in many states, some bars still encourage binge drinking by offering cheap drinks during "Happy Hour."

Such was the case with the Brown-Forman Corporation of Louisville, Kentucky, the second-largest distiller in the United States. On July 19, 1987, a Brown-Forman employee left a company party at which approximately 15 drinks were consumed by each guest. His van crashed head-on into the Volkswagen driven by Don E. Payton. Payton died on the spot, and the employee's blood was found to contain twice the legal limit of alcohol.

Payton's widow subsequently sued both the employee and Brown-Forman, alleging that company policy had encouraged people to consume alcohol before driving and was therefore responsible for her husband's death. Though the employee was sentenced to 20 years imprisonment, he was only made to serve 30 days of his prison term and was then released and put on probation. Brown-Forman, which had been sued for unspecified millions, settled out of court for an undisclosed amount.

Had this case gone to trial and been decided in Mrs. Payton's favor, it would have been the first time a major distiller was held liable for an alcohol-related traffic death. And though the laws vary slightly in each state, this would have strongly reinforced the host liability laws.

Some tow truck drivers offer special discount services to intoxicated bar patrons to assure drivers and their cars safe rides home.

Members of MADD (Mothers Against Drunk Driving) hold pictures of the loved ones they have lost to drunk drivers. MADD has been instrumental in bringing about stringent new drunk driving legislation.

Just as laws vary from state to state, penalties for drunk driving also vary. Predictably, as the legislative assault on drunk driving escalates, so does the severity of penalties imposed for this crime. A checklist in Appendix I shows state-by-state drunk-driving countermeasures in force in 1986 as well as some of the legal deterrents available.

Grass Roots Anger

Grass roots organizations such as Mothers Against Drunk Driving (MADD) have been responsible for bringing about much of the new drunk-driving legislation. MADD was founded in 1980 by Candy Lightner after her 13-year-old daughter Cari was killed by a hit-and-run driver in California. In tracking down her daughter's killer, Ms. Lightner discovered he was out on bail after still another hit-and-run accident. She was appalled to learn about the lenient treatment given many drunk drivers, most of whom never go to jail. Angry and still grieving, she quit her job and started MADD to lobby for new legislation against drunk drivers. MADD's aggressive campaign resulted in California's passing the toughest driving laws then found in the country.

Today MADD is a nationwide nonprofit corporation with half a million supporters and members. There are chapters of MADD in Canada, Great Britain, and New Zealand. According to MADD's central office in Fort Worth, Texas, 400 new drunk-driving laws have been passed in the United States since 1981. As a result of MADD's efforts, media attention, and other citizen-group action, juries are now more sympathetic to the rights of the victim than they are to the rights of the intoxicated driver. MADD believes that strict criminal prosecution of drunk drivers is the most effective deterrent in reducing the menace of drunk driving. The group provides support for drunk-driving victims and continues to lobby for better drunk-driving legislation.

Learning from Other Countries

When the United States finally decided to reform drunk-driving laws, legislators looked abroad to study how successful other countries had been in controlling the problem. They discovered that the United States lagged behind most others in the stringency of its laws. They also saw that they had awakened fairly late to the problem. The rest of the world seemed to have determined many years before that drunk driving could not be tolerated.

The Scandinavian countries Norway and Sweden were the first to take advantage of new scientific methods available to measure blood alcohol levels. As in the United States, old Scandinavian laws had relied on subjective descriptions of intoxicated behavior, on the basis of which judges had been loath to impose fines if no harm had been done. In 1936, Norway established a BAC of .05 as the absolute limit beyond which a driver was legally culpable. Sweden followed in 1941 with two levels of violation, the first between .08 and .14 BAC (later lowered to .05) and the second at .15 BAC. Each level carried a different degree of punishment. Both countries levied severe penalties: loss of license for a year, heavy fines, and/or a month's imprisonment. These laws remain basically the same today, further enforced in 1974 and 1976 by rules allowing police to demand breath tests without restriction at roadblocks.

Norway and Sweden provided a model for other countries to follow. In 1967, led by the lobbying efforts of the

British Medical Association, the British Parliament passed the Road Safety Act. Prior to that time, British laws had been difficult to enforce and did not include BAC measurements, though convicted drivers lost their licenses for a year. The 1967 law set a BAC limit of .08 and allowed police to demand breath tests of traffic violators or obviously impaired drivers. The new legislation brought a storm of controversy, most of it over the breath testing. Because of the controversy, the law made frequent news headlines, heightening everyone's fear that they might be stopped by the police. Perhaps for this reason, road casualties in Britain declined significantly in the months following the law's passage. In 1969, Canada passed legislation similar to Britain's.

France passed a drunk-driving law based on the Scandinavian model in 1978. The French law established a BAC limit of .08 and made breath testing obligatory in any crash. As in Great Britain, there was much debate in France about personal liberty versus public safety. Wine is an important part of French culture, and the beverage industry called the new law a "declaration of war." Despite the controversy, legislators attributed lower crash figures in subsequent months to the effectiveness of the new regulations.

The Netherlands, New Zealand, Australia, and several other countries all have new drunk-driving legislation based more or less on the Scandinavian laws. Not surprising, therefore, is that when the United States got around to passing stronger legislation in the 1980s, American lawmakers borrowed elements from the Norwegian and Swedish models. However, while most American drunk-driving laws continue to be less harsh than those found abroad, they are at least an improvement and an outward sign of legislators' attempts to stem the tide of destruction caused by drunk driving.

Legislators have recently passed stricter penalties for drunk drivers, hoping that license suspensions and jail sentences will deter people from driving while under the influence of alcohol.

CHAPTER 6

EVALUATING THE LAWS

Suppose for a moment that there were no laws to discourage drunk driving. No punishments, no roadblocks, nothing. To what extent would highway fatalities increase? How dangerous would the roads become? Very likely there would be a public outcry demanding protection. It seems obvious to most people that laws are necessary to protect the public from those people who would take advantage of so much freedom. In the absence of internal moral restraints, laws act as a brake upon amoral behavior. Yet it is not clear to what extent drunk-driving laws actually change the behavior of drinking drivers.

Fundamental to all drunk-driving laws is the concept of deterrence. Drunk-driving laws are meant to deter, meaning they should discourage and prevent drinkers from driving. Similarly, the death penalty is intended to deter people from committing murder, not just to punish them. It seems so logical: If there are random roadblocks and stiff penalties, drinkers will not risk taking the wheel. But deterrence works only when human behavior is governed by reason. It has no sway over crimes of passion, it does not always impress alcoholics, and it assumes that for most people the risk of being picked up by the police will outweigh the convenience of driving home.

Thirty percent of the approximately 773,000 drunk drivers arrested annually are repeat offenders. Legislators understand that new, tough drunk-driving laws are probably not going to deter these hard-core drinkers or people who routinely have no respect for laws and highway safety. They do, however, hope that their laws will have an impact on the social drinkers, the majority of the drinking population who report that they have, at some time, driven when they probably should not have.

Of course, deterrence is only part of the job of better drunk-driving legislation. Jail sentences and suspended licenses get dangerous drivers off the road. Heavy fines boost the highway budget. Mandatory detoxification programs may put some alcoholics on the road to recovery. But without massive expenditures of manpower and money, the police can arrest and convict relatively few drunk drivers. Therefore, law enforcement officials hope that drunk-driving laws can do some of their work for them, by deterring the trouble before it starts. They hope that a lively public awareness of the laws will alert everyone to the serious risks and penalties of drunk driving.

To this end, most new drunk-driving laws are greeted with a flurry of media attention. Newspapers and local television stations devote extra space and time to explanations of the new regulations. Newspaper editorials endorse them and urge the public to take them seriously. Often, enactment of the laws is timed to coincide with a holiday period, such as Christmas, when the risk of drunk-driving accidents is greatest. Usually, highway police make an extra show of force in the months following passage of the laws, setting up roadblocks to demonstrate that they mean business. Arrests and convictions usually go up. Then everyone waits to see whether the laws will really make a difference, whether fatalities will go down, and whether drinking/driving behavior will change.

Scandinavia: A Valid Model?

Presumably, Scandinavia's drunk-driving laws must have been quite effective to have been emulated by so many countries. Traffic experts in Norway and Sweden claimed their laws worked well, and other countries assumed they were adopt-

A cartoon takes a biting look at the leniency with which some judges and law enforcement officials treat drunk drivers.

ing a model that had proved successful. In fact, however, the Scandinavian laws had not yet been scientifically evaluated at the time of their adoption by other countries.

Evaluation of most drunk-driving laws is extremely difficult because so many factors must be considered. World events, a nation's driving and drinking habits, driving experience, economic conditions, highway conditions, and the amount of publicity or controversy surrounding the new laws all can augment or diminish their impact. In 1936 and 1941, when Norway and Sweden passed their drunk-driving laws, World War II and events leading up to it were crowding out other headlines, so the laws received little publicity. Both countries had poor roads and inexperienced drivers, and both already had fairly strong drunk-driving laws.

Not surprisingly, therefore, highway fatalities in Norway and Sweden in the years before and after the 1936 and 1941 legislation remained about the same. Scandinavian traffic experts could point to relatively low accident rates in their countries because drinking and driving had been relatively uncommon in their countries all along, that is, the low rates were not the result of any legal effort. Sadly, highway fatalities increased dramatically in Norway and Sweden after World War II as the number of licensed drivers increased.

But this does not mean that drunk-driving laws have had no long-term deterrent effect in Scandinavia. Nighttime road-side surveys of Scandinavian drivers report no more than 2.7% of drivers with illegal blood alcohol concentrations. Some surveys find less than 1%. By comparison, 7–10% of American nighttime drivers have illegal BAC concentrations.

Drunk driving by problem drinkers or those undeterred by any laws is still a concern in Scandinavia. But among a substantial portion of the population there is an impressive consensus that driving after drinking is unacceptable, risky behavior. Just how much this consensus owes to cultural factors and how much to drunk-driving legislation would be difficult to determine.

It is interesting to note, however, that although the drunk-driving laws are well known in Scandinavia and taken quite seriously by most people, police in Norway and Sweden actually stop relatively few drivers. The chances of being punished for drunk driving are not much greater there than they would be in the United States.

The United Kingdom: An Active Deterrent

The British Road Safety Act of 1967 was a bit easier to evaluate than the drunk-driving legislation in Scandinavia. Traffic records in the United Kingdom were more detailed, and no other legislation or world events competed for attention. The 1973 fuel crisis, which radically altered driving habits, was still a number of years away. The Road Safety Act was well publicized, largely because of the controversy it created.

The controversy centered on the act's provisions for random breath testing by police. Initially, the law would have allowed police to stop anyone and demand a breath test. But to many people this seemed a violation of individual civil rights. Random breath testing was unprecedented at that time, even in Scandinavia. The law was revised to permit police to test only those drivers involved in an accident, committing a traffic violation, or strongly suspected of being drunk. Even so, many police officers and judges objected, arguing that the law contained too many loopholes and entailed too much paperwork.

In the years immediately following passage of the Road Safety Act in Britain, fatalities and serious injuries did decrease in number. There was an initial decline in traffic deaths of 24.7%, signifying that the new legislation was having a positive deterrent effect. Unfortunately, the results did not last beyond three years. The British public gradually realized that they had overestimated the threat of police apprehension. Police were, in fact, reluctant to enforce the law. The chances of being tested were about 1 in 2 million miles in 1970. Gradually the law lost all its original power.

In 1975, a determined police chief in Cheshire, England, decided to test whether a concentrated period of rigorous enforcement of the 1967 law would have much impact. For one week in July his police officers carried out alcohol breath tests on all drivers involved in accidents or traffic violations. Then well-publicized testing was extended for the entire month of September. Traffic accidents dropped dramatically for the week in July and for September. The Cheshire "blitz" proved that the 1967 law could have a deterrent effect, but only when it was rigorously enforced and widely publicized.

The United States: Following Britain's Pattern

In the United States, drunk-driving laws are often as difficult to evaluate as in Europe. Generally, however, a pattern emerges that echoes the British experience. When laws are well publicized and enforced, they are successful; when those elements are lacking, they fail.

For example, the state of Maine passed new drunk-driving legislation in 1981, one of the first states to do so after California. The new law established an illegal BAC at .10, doubled many penalties, and increased the chances of a DWI conviction. It specified a mandatory two-day jail sentence for first offenders and all repeat offenders. In the first year following passage of the law, traffic fatalities in Maine dropped by approximately one-third. Three years later, as the public's perception of the law's threat weakened, traffic fatalities returned to prelaw levels. Similar results were recorded in Mas-

A liqueur ad juxtaposed with a call for stricter treatment of drunk drivers. Alcohol use is so widely accepted in our society that many people still do not take the dangers of drunk driving seriously.

sachusetts, New Mexico, and Minnesota following passage of new drunk-driving laws.

It is easier to publicize drunk-driving laws than to enforce them. In order to be effective, they require substantial endorsement by, and commitment on the part of, police and judges. But many new laws are controversial or hard to understand. Police feel overworked by extra paperwork and time-consuming roadside arrests. Lawyers obtain light sentences for their clients from indifferent judges. Trials back up in court, and sentences are imposed too slowly or cases dismissed entirely. In Massachusetts, for example, as many as 2,000 drunk-driving cases a year are dismissed when police fail to show up to testify in court. When the police and the courts do manage to carry out the laws, their efforts must be sustained over a long period of time. Otherwise, the drinking public perceives the laws as only a distant threat.

What drunk-driving penalties are most effective and easiest to enforce? Many experts would say that loss of license is as effective a deterrent as any. They would add that the license should be suspended immediately to have maximum impact, preferably at the side of the road by the arresting officer on the basis of breath-analysis results. Though roadside arrest is time-consuming for the police, it saves later court time, gets dangerous drivers off the road, and ensures that they are penalized. It causes great inconvenience for a driver and is a punishment well suited to the crime, because it is a reminder that a driver's license is a privilege. The law implies that anyone driving drunk should forfeit a privilege so flagrantly abused. Once considered a radical measure and called unconstitutional, "administrative license pickup" is the law today in an increasing number of states.

Safe Highways Save Lives

Some of the most effective highway legislation is not directed specifically at drunk drivers but rather at making the roads safer for everyone. Moderate speed limits, safer cars, and better-lit and well-leveled roads fit this category of legislation. So do seat-belt laws, in force in many states. During the years 1982–84, seat belts had been worn by only 6% of those who died in highway accidents. It has been estimated that if all states had mandatory seat-belt laws (about half the states now do) and if the laws were respected and enforced, approximately 4,000 lives could be saved nationwide each year.

Though legislation to curb drunk driving can go a long way toward saving the lives of drinking drivers and their innocent victims alike, the law alone cannot solve the problem. Making the public aware of the dangers of drinking and driving is also necessary. To further this aim, many grass roots organizations have taken it upon themselves to educate the public — parents and teenagers alike — about the deadly combination of alcohol and automobiles.

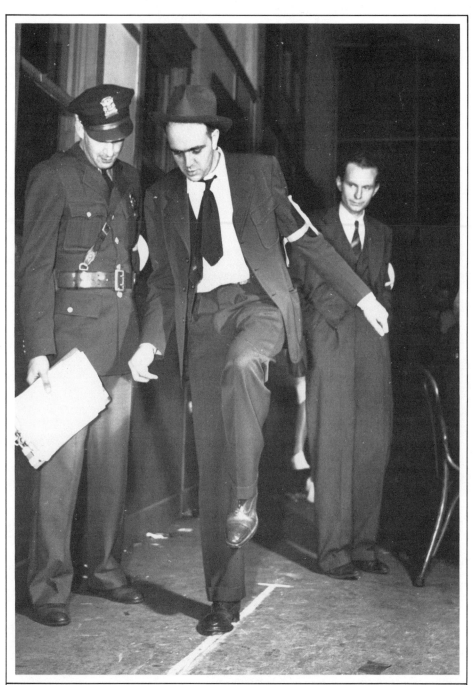

In the 1940s, sobriety tests involved little more than being made to walk a straight line. In the 1980s, more sophisticated methods, such as blood tests and breath analyses, are employed.

CHAPTER 7

OLD PROBLEMS, NEW SOLUTIONS

Nearly every psychoactive drug has been abused at some time in history. Tobacco smoking was rampant in Europe in the 18th century. In the 19th century, millions of Chinese succumbed to opium addiction. Cocaine caused addiction among many 19th-century doctors and their patients. But most of the victims of this abuse were the drug users themselves. The drunk on horseback endangered no one but himself. If the tipsy rider could just manage to keep himself in the saddle, the horse could probably find its way back to the barn.

In contrast, driving drunk or under the influence of drugs at high speeds on superhighways is a uniquely modern problem that endangers everyone. Even a few generations ago, the drunk-driving crisis was not as acute as it is now. Fewer young people owned cars or drank alcohol, and highway speeds were slower. Most cars were larger or heavier and, to some degree, safer than they are today. So while alcohol abuse may be an old problem, the times we live in demand new solutions.

Today's challenge to curb drunk driving requires the efforts of all levels of society, from individuals to government, from private community organizations to the automobile and liquor industries. Special attention must be paid to the teens who are drinking and driving. Steps have already been taken in this direction, but there is still a long way to go. Young drinking drivers used to be assigned by the courts to programs more appropriate for adult problem drinkers. Educators and law enforcement officials gradually realized that young drinkers needed programs designed for them. The many programs that now exist are also new — too new to evaluate their long-term effectiveness. Most people realize that the problem is more complicated and difficult to solve than they had once imagined. Frightening films like *The Last Prom* or *One for the Road*, showing crumpled, twisted cars, bodies heaved into ambulances, and weeping parents, are not enough. Neither are most in-school drug-education courses, but at least they can provide the foundation needed to educate teens about the dangers of substance abuse.

Most experts now agree that elementary school is not too early to begin teaching children about drunk driving and its attendant problems.

Boy Scouts enjoy a snack at a meeting. The scouting movement has been successful in providing an antidrug peer group for its members.

Education: Arming Children for the Future

Ninety-three percent of junior high and high schools today offer some kind of drug education. Some of these programs run for a full semester or academic year and are quite thorough. Others last only a week or two. Too often teachers are not properly trained to teach the information offered in these courses or have ambivalent feelings about drugs. In any case, most students say they get their drug information outside of school, from friends and older brothers and sisters. The challenge for educators is to reach students early, before they have become misinformed and have developed bad habits and the attitude that drugs are "cool." Therefore, at its most worthwhile, today's drug-education curriculum begins in elementary school.

What can little children possibly understand about drugs? The *Here's Looking at You, Too* curriculum provides an example. Developed in Seattle, Washington, it begins with kindergarten and runs through twelfth grade. Kindergarten and first-grade students learn problem-solving skills and skills for coping with stress. Using puppets and stories, they explore alternative ways to solve problems and acceptable ways to express their feelings. Second- and third-grade students study the effects of using and abusing alcohol and other drugs. Fourth-grade students learn the difference between over-the-counter drugs and prescription drugs. Fifth-graders study why people use drugs and alcohol. Sixth-graders discuss parental attitudes and learn where they can turn for help when they need it.

Trying to Stem the Flow of Fatalities

There are many organizations and programs designed to help teenagers — junior high or high school students — avoid the dangers of drunk driving. Many seek to conquer peer pressure; others simply offer an alternative to getting behind the wheel of a car.

Students Against Driving Drunk (SADD) is one of the most active and well-known organizations enlisted in the war against teenage drunk driving. It was founded in the early 1980s by a Massachusetts high school teacher and athletic coach named Robert Anastas, who was appalled by the death and mutilation caused by mixing alcohol and automobiles, and decided to do something about it. SADD takes the position that the best defense against the carnage on the highways among adolescent drunk drivers is to educate young people about the dangers involved. SADD also emphasizes that it is against the law for teens to drink alcohol and stresses that this alone should be a compelling reason for them to avoid doing so.

Having made this position clear, however, SADD recognizes that on occasion teens will drink even to the point of intoxication. At that point, it is crucial to keep them from getting behind the wheel of a car. SADD has devised a contract to be signed by young people and their parents in which the teenager agrees to call his parents for a ride home if he or the person on whom he is depending for a ride has been drinking. In turn, the parent agrees to postpone any discussion about the drinking until a later time. Robert Anastas calls this contract a "safeguard against death." The SADD contract has been commended for saving lives and encouraging dialogue between young people and their parents. Although SADD has been criticized by some people for seeming to condone teenage drinking, the organization's point is that while underage drinking in *not* to be sanctioned, those who indulge in it should not be made to pay for their mistake with their lives.

At CASPAR, the Massachusetts-based counseling program for children of alcoholics, a peer-education program developed as an offshoot of the general Alcohol Education Program (AEP). The organization, which had used high school students as teacher assistants in AEP, soon recognized their potential. Each year students from neighboring schools are encouraged to apply to become peer leaders, and those selected receive 40–60 hours of training during the summer, followed by a peer-leader test. In the fall they are ready to lead small after-school discussion groups at the comfortable

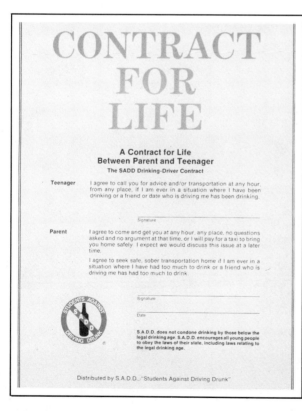

CONTRACT FOR LIFE

**A Contract for Life
Between Parent and Teenager**
The SADD Drinking-Driver Contract

Teenager — I agree to call you for advice and/or transportation at any hour, from any place, if I am ever in a situation where I have been drinking or a friend or date who is driving me has been drinking.

Signature

Parent — I agree to come and get you at any hour, any place, no questions asked and no argument at that time, or I will pay for a taxi to bring you home safely. I expect we would discuss this issue at a later time.

I agree to seek safe, sober transportation home if I am ever in a situation where I have had too much to drink or a friend who is driving me has had too much to drink.

Signature

Date

S.A.D.D. does not condone drinking by those below the legal drinking age. S.A.D.D. encourages all young people to obey the laws of their state, including laws relating to the legal drinking age.

Distributed by S.A.D.D., "Students Against Driving Drunk"

The contract devised by Students Against Driving Drunk has been commended for saving lives and opening lines of communication between parents and their teenage children.

old home that is CASPAR's headquarters. Peer leaders and group members get paid for the hours they put into the program, and CASPAR counselors say the results seem worthwhile.

Project Graduation is another peer-centered program, one focused specifically on eliminating alcohol-related fatalities. Project Graduation began in Maine, following a 1979 commencement season in which there were 12 highway deaths among teenagers. The focus of Project Graduation is to create appealing and entertaining graduation parties at which no alcohol is served and to engage the support and concern of the school and community for such events. In most schools, a team of students, teachers, and parents plan the event, and the entire community becomes involved in fund-raising and publicity. There have been no alcohol-related highway fatalities in Maine since 1980 in those communities that have adopted the Project Graduation plan for drug- and alcohol-free parties. Since 1980, 129 Maine high schools have started Project Graduation celebrations, as have more than a dozen other schools across the country.

The Just Say No program is aimed primarily at junior-high age students. It seeks to create peer pressure not to use drugs and to enable young people to resist temptation. "Role play" situations enable "Just Say No" members to develop effective strategies for turning their backs on alcohol and drugs wherever and whenever they are exposed to these substances. One "say no" process might be as follows:

1. Ask questions.

2. Name the trouble.

3. Identify the consequences.

4. Suggest an alternative.

5. Leave, but leave the door open for further communication.

In a drinking/driving situation, this process might be acted out this way: You are offered a ride home by someone who has been drinking. You might ask how much they have had to drink. If they admit they have had several drinks or you suspect it, you can recognize the risk: "That's going to triple my chances of an accident." You can identify the consequences for yourself and the driver: risk of an accident, revocation of license if caught, disapproval of family and friends. Then you can suggest an alternative: "My Dad won't mind picking us up," or, "Let's ask Tony to drive us home; he hasn't been drinking." If your choices are rejected, seek other transportation for yourself and get help from peers and adults to prevent the drunk driver from driving.

Another program based on positive peer group reinforcement is the Green Mountain Prevention Project in Vermont. Each summer it gathers 120 participants from 40 schools around the state for a 5-day peer training program. The participants are urged to form workshops and discussion groups in their home communities, sharing what they have learned during the summer. Above all, they become positive role models for their friends and classmates.

Another program, this one in Lafayette, California, is called NEAT (New Experiences in Affection and Trust). NEAT's stated goals are to stop drug abuse, provide peer support, and promote health. Teens provide weekly support through a network of phone calls and operate a roadside produce stand in the summer.

An entirely different kind of program targeted at high-risk drinkers has been established in Baltimore, Maryland. Called the Adolescent Trauma Prevention Program, it organizes groups of young first offenders (ages 13 to 18) or heavy drinkers and drug users for visits to an area shock trauma unit that treats crash victims from all over Maryland. At the trauma unit, participants talk with patients who themselves may have been heavy drug users. They also meet patients who are still significantly impaired after several years of hospitalization and surgery. The trauma-unit visit is one of six sessions, two of which are attended by parents. Understandably, many of the young people are visibly shaken by the trauma unit visit, and memories of the visit are vivid months later. In a six-month follow-up, 79% of the participants claimed the program had had a positive impact on their alcohol or drug problems.

There are hundreds of similar drug-prevention programs providing peer support around the country. SADD is one of the most successful. The Boy Scouts, who have been encouraging their Explorer members to be role models and peer leaders in drug prevention, is another. Most of the programs are too new to evaluate their success. Some participants and counselors express discouragement about the magnitude of the problem and despair that some young people seem almost indifferent about their futures. But something — perhaps these programs — is getting the message across. Young people themselves probably deserve much of the credit for helping highway fatalities go down in the 1980s.

Government and Industry: The Larger Picture

To be sure, the decision of whether to drink and drive is ultimately up to the individual, who must take responsibility for the consequences of his or her actions. However, federal, state, and local governments have enormous power to influence individual decisions about drinking. So does the alcohol-beverage industry itself. One obvious deterrent to drinking

In an effort to combat the drunk driving problem, the Seagram Company has created a public service campaign warning people not to drive if they have had "one too many."

would be to make it more expensive. Alcohol is still taxed at the same rate as it was in 1950, at about $1.25 a gallon. Other commodities, such as gasoline, are now taxed at a much higher rate than alcohol.

Another deterrent is to raise the drinking age, which has been done in many states. A more radical solution might be to place labels warning of possible addiction on all alcoholic beverages, similar to the warning labels on cigarettes, or to ban all alcohol commercials from television. After a DWI conviction, the driver's license might read "alcoholic," just as many specify, "Must wear corrective lenses for vision." The sale of alcohol could be prohibited near major highways.

What about the automobile industry's responsibility for making safer cars? Can our highways be better lit and better designed? Should beer be so easily available at gas stations and roadside convenience stores? Can public transportation be improved near large stadiums, parks, and theaters, where beer, wine, and alcohol are frequently sold, thus eliminating reliance on private cars?

There are some hopeful indications. For example, since 1948 the Seagram liquor company has sponsored research to improve detection of drunk drivers. The company also runs public-service advertisements urging its customers not to overindulge. Public awareness is at a new height, thanks to anti–drunk driving organizations, media campaigns, and stricter law enforcement. Alcohol-related deaths have declined, even though the number of licensed drivers has increased. Highway fatalities declined from 51,000 deaths in 1980 to 43,000 in 1985. Surveys in some states show a small decline in "binge" drinking. A 1985 Gallup poll suggests that Americans are drinking about 5% less than in the 1970s.

But the optimism is hedged with caution. A major Crime Institute study points out that most drunk drivers who cause fatal accidents are not even tested for alcohol abuse. The study suggests that the statistics on drunk driving are misleading and inaccurate and that alcohol and other drugs are responsible for many more accidents than police reports indicate. New, well-publicized, harsher penalties for drunk driving tend to have only a short-term effect. Efforts to improve public transportation move slowly for a nation still in love with Henry Ford's invention—the private automobile.

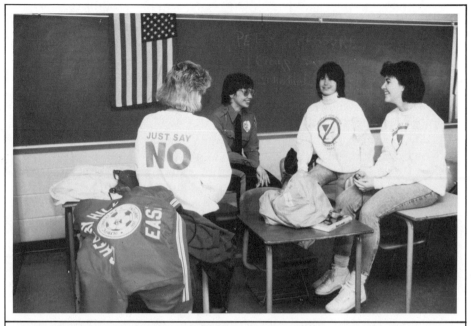

Students discuss an antidrug campaign with a police officer. It is hoped that such programs will turn the tide on teenage drunk driving.

The Bottom Line

Suppose all the possible solutions worked and drunk driving were a thing of the past. How many lives would be saved? Some estimate that there would be a 24% reduction in traffic deaths. That would mean 11,000–13,000 lives would be saved annually. Others say that drinking is involved in 50–90% of all fatal accidents. Traffic statistics are open to different interpretations, and it is hard to verify such estimates. However, most people would agree that though traffic accidents and fatalities would still be high, if drunk driving were to become a thing of the past, a significant number of lives would be saved.

Although the public turned its back on the drunk-driving problem for a long time, today it has focused its attention on this issue. The drunk driver is no longer perceived as a sympathetic figure but as a public menace. The message appears everywhere — at restaurants, in parking garages, on bumper stickers, and even printed on computerized paychecks —

"Don't drink and drive." This awareness is paying off: In 1986, Transportation Secretary Elizabeth Dole reported that the percentage of people who died on the nation's highways had dropped to its lowest level in history. Alcohol-related traffic fatalities had declined by 25%. Unfortunately, recent national legislation to raise the highway speed limit and decisions in some states to eliminate seat-belt laws may reverse this trend.

A closer look at current traffic figures shows that young people still make up too high a percentage of the death toll. Will public awareness of the problem and the vigorous efforts of private and government drunk-driving programs continue to keep fatalities down? They must. Otherwise, young people will not often get arrested for drunk driving; they will simply die.

APPENDIX I

Crime and Punishment

Laws and penalties for drunk driving vary considerably from state to state. However, the trend nationwide is toward stricter punishments. The following is a representative sampling of the legal countermeasures to drunk driving available throughout the United States as of 1986.

Crime: DWI, first offense.

For minor:

• Penalty: loss of provisional youth license ("learner's permit") for 30 to 90 days. Suspension may be immediate ("roadside surrender"), by arresting officer.
• Referral to special youth alcohol education program or mandatory attendance in such a program.
• Community service.
• Fines.

For adults:

• Penalty: mandatory loss of license for 30 to 90 days. Suspension may be immediate, by arresting officer.
• Fines, averaging $75 to $200.
• Mandatory attendance at detoxification classes in or out of prison.
• Community service.

Crime: DWI, second offense.

• Penalty: Jail sentence, 7 to 90 days minimum; days served consecutively or on weekends. Some sentences served at a residential alcohol-treatment center. This sentence may be mandatory if second conviction comes within six months of the first.
• Fines, $75 to $1,000.
• Loss of license for 30 to 90 days. Suspension may be immediate, by arresting officer.
• Mandatory attendance at detoxification classes in or out of prison. Failure to attend classes may result in minimum two-day jail sentence.
• Community service.
• House arrest.

Crime: refusal to take breathalyzer test.

• Penalty: automatic loss of license/learner's permit for 30 to 120 days. Refusal to take test can be used as evidence in court.

Crime: crash, DWI, and vehicular homicide or injury.

A vehicular homicide caused by DWI is designated as a felony in most states.

• Penalty: mandatory six-month minimum jail sentence. All DWI penalties as above. No option of serving time in alcohol-education program instead of in jail.

Crime: driving with suspended or revoked license.

• Penalty: mandatory jail sentence, with length of sentence varying from 30 to 90 days.

In some states, several of these penalties will be levied for the same crime; in other states, only one or two penalties will be levied. In addition to these penalties, nearly every community newspaper prints the names of those arrested for drunk driving.

APPENDIX II

State Agencies for the Prevention and Treatment of Drug Abuse

ALABAMA
Department of Mental Health
Division of Mental Illness and
  Substance Abuse Community
  Programs
200 Interstate Park Drive
P.O. Box 3710
Montgomery, AL 36193
(205) 271-9253

ALASKA
Department of Health and Social
  Services
Office of Alcoholism and Drug
  Abuse
Pouch H-05-F
Juneau, AK 99811
(907) 586-6201

ARIZONA
Department of Health Services
Division of Behavioral Health
  Services
Bureau of Community Services
Alcohol Abuse and Alcoholism
  Section
2500 East Van Buren
Phoenix, AZ 85008
(602) 255-1238

Department of Health Services
Division of Behavioral Health
  Services
Bureau of Community Services
Drug Abuse Section
2500 East Van Buren
Phoenix, AZ 85008
(602) 255-1240

ARKANSAS
Department of Human Services
Office of Alcohol and Drug Abuse
  Prevention
1515 West 7th Avenue
Suite 310
Little Rock, AR 72202
(501) 371-2603

CALIFORNIA
Department of Alcohol and Drug
  Abuse
111 Capitol Mall
Sacramento, CA 95814
(916) 445-1940

COLORADO
Department of Health
Alcohol and Drug Abuse Division
4210 East 11th Avenue
Denver, CO 80220
(303) 320-6137

CONNECTICUT
Alcohol and Drug Abuse
  Commission
999 Asylum Avenue
3rd Floor
Hartford, CT 06105
(203) 566-4145

DELAWARE
Division of Mental Health
Bureau of Alcoholism and Drug
  Abuse
1901 North Dupont Highway
Newcastle, DE 19720
(302) 421-6101

DISTRICT OF COLUMBIA
Department of Human Services
Office of Health Planning and
  Development
601 Indiana Avenue, NW
Suite 500
Washington, D.C. 20004
(202) 724-5641

FLORIDA
Department of Health and
  Rehabilitative Services
Alcoholic Rehabilitation Program
1317 Winewood Boulevard
Room 187A
Tallahassee, FL 32301
(904) 488-0396

Department of Health and
  Rehabilitative Services
Drug Abuse Program
1317 Winewood Boulevard
Building 6, Room 155
Tallahassee, FL 32301
(904) 488-0900

GEORGIA
Department of Human Resources
Division of Mental Health and
  Mental Retardation
Alcohol and Drug Section
618 Ponce De Leon Avenue, NE
Atlanta, GA 30365-2101
(404) 894-4785

HAWAII
Department of Health
Mental Health Division
Alcohol and Drug Abuse Branch
1250 Punch Bowl Street
P.O. Box 3378
Honolulu, HI 96801
(808) 548-4280

IDAHO
Department of Health and Welfare
Bureau of Preventive Medicine
Substance Abuse Section
450 West State
Boise, ID 83720
(208) 334-4368

ILLINOIS
Department of Mental Health and
  Developmental Disabilities
Division of Alcoholism
160 North La Salle Street
Room 1500
Chicago, IL 60601
(312) 793-2907

Illinois Dangerous Drugs
  Commission
300 North State Street
Suite 1500
Chicago, IL 60610
(312) 822-9860

INDIANA
Department of Mental Health
Division of Addiction Services
429 North Pennsylvania Street
Indianapolis, IN 46204
(317) 232-7816

IOWA
Department of Substance Abuse
505 5th Avenue
Insurance Exchange Building
Suite 202
Des Moines, IA 50319
(515) 281-3641

KANSAS
Department of Social Rehabilitation
Alcohol and Drug Abuse Services
2700 West 6th Street
Biddle Building
Topeka, KS 66606
(913) 296-3925

KENTUCKY
Cabinet for Human Resources
Department of Health Services
Substance Abuse Branch
275 East Main Street
Frankfort, KY 40601
(502) 564-2880

LOUISIANA
Department of Health and Human
  Resources
Office of Mental Health and
  Substance Abuse
655 North 5th Street
P.O. Box 4049
Baton Rouge, LA 70821
(504) 342-2565

MAINE
Department of Human Services
Office of Alcoholism and Drug
  Abuse Prevention
Bureau of Rehabilitation
32 Winthrop Street
Augusta, ME 04330
(207) 289-2781

MARYLAND
Alcoholism Control Administration
201 West Preston Street
Fourth Floor
Baltimore, MD 21201
(301) 383-2977

State Health Department
Drug Abuse Administration
201 West Preston Street
Baltimore, MD 21201
(301) 383-3312

MASSACHUSETTS
Department of Public Health
Division of Alcoholism
755 Boylston Street
Sixth Floor
Boston, MA 02116
(617) 727-1960

Department of Public Health
Division of Drug Rehabilitation
600 Washington Street
Boston, MA 02114
(617) 727-8617

MICHIGAN
Department of Public Health
Office of Substance Abuse Services
3500 North Logan Street
P.O. Box 30035
Lansing, MI 48909
(517) 373-8603

MINNESOTA
Department of Public Welfare
Chemical Dependency Program
  Division
Centennial Building
658 Cedar Street
4th Floor
Saint Paul, MN 55155
(612) 296-4614

MISSISSIPPI
Department of Mental Health
Division of Alcohol and Drug Abuse
1102 Robert E. Lee Building
Jackson, MS 39201
(601) 359-1297

MISSOURI
Department of Mental Health
Division of Alcoholism and Drug
  Abuse
2002 Missouri Boulevard
P.O. Box 687
Jefferson City, MO 65102
(314) 751-4942

MONTANA
Department of Institutions
Alcohol and Drug Abuse Division
1539 11th Avenue
Helena, MT 59620
(406) 449-2827

NEBRASKA
Department of Public Institutions
Division of Alcoholism and Drug
Abuse
801 West Van Dorn Street
P.O. Box 94728
Lincoln, NB 68509
(402) 471-2851, Ext. 415

NEVADA
Department of Human Resources
Bureau of Alcohol and Drug Abuse
505 East King Street
Carson City, NV 89710
(702) 885-4790

NEW HAMPSHIRE
Department of Health and Welfare
Office of Alcohol and Drug Abuse
    Prevention
Hazen Drive
Health and Welfare Building
Concord, NH 03301
(603) 271-4627

NEW JERSEY
Department of Health
Division of Alcoholism
129 East Hanover Street CN 362
Trenton, NJ 08625
(609) 292-8949

Department of Health
Division of Narcotic and Drug
    Abuse Control
129 East Hanover Street CN 362
Trenton, NJ 08625
(609) 292-8949

NEW MEXICO
Health and Environment Department
Behavioral Services Division
Substance Abuse Bureau
725 Saint Michaels Drive
P.O. Box 968
Santa Fe, NM 87503
(505) 984-0020, Ext. 304

NEW YORK
Division of Alcoholism and Alcohol
    Abuse
194 Washington Avenue
Albany, NY 12210
(518) 474-5417

Division of Substance Abuse
    Services
Executive Park South
Box 8200
Albany, NY 12203
(518) 457-7629

NORTH CAROLINA
Department of Human Resources
Division of Mental Health, Mental
    Retardation and Substance Abuse
    Services
Alcohol and Drug Abuse Services
325 North Salisbury Street
Albemarle Building
Raleigh, NC 27611
(919) 733-4670

NORTH DAKOTA
Department of Human Services
Division of Alcoholism and Drug
    Abuse
State Capitol Building
Bismarck, ND 58505
(701) 224-2767

OHIO
Department of Health
Division of Alcoholism
246 North High Street
P.O. Box 118
Columbus, OH 43216
(614) 466-3543

Department of Mental Health
Bureau of Drug Abuse
65 South Front Street
Columbus, OH 43215
(614) 466-9023

OKLAHOMA
Department of Mental Health
Alcohol and Drug Programs
4545 North Lincoln Boulevard
Suite 100 East Terrace
P.O. Box 53277
Oklahoma City, OK 73152
(405) 521-0044

OREGON
Department of Human Resources
Mental Health Division
Office of Programs for Alcohol and
Drug Problems
2575 Bittern Street, NE
Salem, OR 97310
(503) 378-2163

PENNSYLVANIA
Department of Health
Office of Drug and Alcohol
Programs
Commonwealth and Forster Avenues
Health and Welfare Building
P.O. Box 90
Harrisburg, PA 17108
(717) 787-9857

RHODE ISLAND
Department of Mental Health,
Mental Retardation and Hospitals
Division of Substance Abuse
Substance Abuse Administration
Building
Cranston, RI 02920
(401) 464-2091

SOUTH CAROLINA
Commission on Alcohol and Drug
Abuse
3700 Forest Drive
Columbia, SC 29204
(803) 758-2521

SOUTH DAKOTA
Department of Health
Division of Alcohol and Drug Abuse
523 East Capitol, Joe Foss Building
Pierre, SD 57501
(605) 773-4806

TENNESSEE
Department of Mental Health and
Mental Retardation
Alcohol and Drug Abuse Services
505 Deaderick Street
James K. Polk Building,
Fourth Floor
Nashville, TN 37219
(615) 741-1921

TEXAS
Commission on Alcoholism
809 Sam Houston State Office
Building
Austin, TX 78701
(512) 475-2577
Department of Community Affairs
Drug Abuse Prevention Division
2015 South Interstate Highway 35
P.O. Box 13166
Austin, TX 78711
(512) 443-4100

UTAH
Department of Social Services
Division of Alcoholism and Drugs
150 West North Temple
Suite 350
P.O. Box 2500
Salt Lake City, UT 84110
(801) 533-6532

VERMONT
Agency of Human Services
Department of Social and
Rehabilitation Services
Alcohol and Drug Abuse Division
103 South Main Street
Waterbury, VT 05676
(802) 241-2170

VIRGINIA
Department of Mental Health and
  Mental Retardation
Division of Substance Abuse
109 Governor Street
P.O. Box 1797
Richmond, VA 23214
(804) 786-5313

WASHINGTON
Department of Social and Health
  Service
Bureau of Alcohol and Substance
  Abuse
Office Building—44 W
Olympia, WA 98504
(206) 753-5866

WEST VIRGINIA
Department of Health
Office of Behavioral Health Services
Division on Alcoholism and Drug
  Abuse
1800 Washington Street East
Building 3 Room 451
Charleston, WV 25305
(304) 348-2276

WISCONSIN
Department of Health and Social
  Services
Division of Community Services
Bureau of Community Programs
Alcohol and Other Drug Abuse
  Program Office
1 West Wilson Street
P.O. Box 7851
Madison, WI 53707
(608) 266-2717

WYOMING
Alcohol and Drug Abuse Programs
Hathaway Building
Cheyenne, WY 82002
(307) 777-7115, Ext. 7118

GUAM
Mental Health & Substance Abuse
  Agency
P.O. Box 20999
Guam 96921

PUERTO RICO
Department of Addiction Control
  Services
Alcohol Abuse Programs
P.O. Box B-Y Rio Piedras Station
Rio Piedras, PR 00928
(809) 763-5014

Department of Addiction Control
  Services
Drug Abuse Programs
P.O. Box B-Y Rio Piedras Station
Rio Piedras, PR 00928
(809) 764-8140

VIRGIN ISLANDS
Division of Mental Health,
  Alcoholism & Drug Dependency
  Services
P.O. Box 7329
Saint Thomas, Virgin Islands 00801
(809) 774-7265

AMERICAN SAMOA
LBJ Tropical Medical Center
Department of Mental Health Clinic
Pago Pago, American Samoa 96799

TRUST TERRITORIES
Director of Health Services
Office of the High Commissioner
Saipan, Trust Territories 96950

Further Reading

Anastas, Robert. *The Contract for Life — The Story of S.A.D.D.* New York: Pocket Books, 1986.

Cross, Wilbur. *Kids and Booze: What You Must Know to Help Them*. New York: Dutton, 1979.

Dusek, Dorothy, and Daniel A. Girdano. *Drugs: A Factual Account*. Reading, MA: Addison-Wesley, 1980.

Goode, Erich. *Drugs in American Society*. New York: Knopf, 1984.

Ross, H. Lawrence. *Deterring the Drinking Driver: Legal Policy and Social Control*. Lexington, MA: Lexington Books, 1984.

Silverstein, Alvin, M.D., and Virginia Silverstein. *Alcoholism*. Philadelphia: Lippincott, 1975.

Glossary

addiction a condition caused by repeated drug use, characterized by a compulsive urge to continue using the drug, a tendency to increase dosage, and physiological and/or psychological dependence

alcoholism alcohol abuse causing deterioration in health and social relations

amphetamine any one of a number of drugs that act to stimulate parts of the central nervous system

barbiturate any one of a number of drugs that cause depression of the central nervous system; generally used to reduce anxiety or induce euphoria

blackout a temporary loss of consciousness

blood-alcohol concentration the percentage of alcohol in the bloodstream

cerebral cortex the area of the brain responsible for judgment, self-control, and reason; first area affected by alcohol

cocaine the primary psychoactive ingredient in the coca plant; it functions as a behavioral stimulant

depressant a drug that depresses the central nervous system; examples include barbiturates and tranquilizers, which are used to help people block out unpleasant thoughts or anxieties and reduce tension

DWI driving while intoxicated; one of the leading causes of death among young people

over-the-counter drugs nonprescription drugs such as allergy pills and cold syrups

peer pressure the pressure to do something that may not be right or feel natural just to be a part of a group

physical dependence adaptation of the body to the presence of a drug such that its absence produces withdrawal symptoms

psychoactive chemically affecting the mind or behavior

psychological dependence a condition in which the drug user craves a drug to maintain a sense of well-being and feels discomfort when deprived of it

sedative a drug that induces feelings of increased relaxation at first, eventually leading to sluggishness and lack of motor coordination; some sedatives are barbiturates and tranquilizers

stimulant any drug that increases brain activity and produces the sensation of greater energy, euphoria, and increased alertness

THC tetrahydrocannabinol, the chief psychoactive chemical in marijuana

tolerance a decrease in susceptibility to the effects of a drug due to its continued administration, resulting in the user's need to increase the drug dosage to achieve the effects experienced previously

tranquilizer an antianxiety drug that has calming and relaxing effects; Librium and Valium are tranquilizers

withdrawal the physiological and psychological effects of discontinued use of a drug

PICTURE CREDITS

AP/Wide World Photos: pp. 50, 71, 75, 84; Art Resource: p. 8; BACCHUS/
University of Kentucky: p. 40; The Bettmann Archive: p. 12; The Comprehensive Care Corporation: pp. 29, 31, 48, 56; Laimute Druskis/Taurus
Photos: p. 55; Freelance Photographers Guild: p. 24; The House of Seagram: p. 94; Iowa Department of Public Health/Division of Substance
Abuse: p. 37; Eric Kroll/Taurus Photos: pp. 34, 52; New York State Liquor Authority: p. 68; Nisa Rauschenberg: p. 73; Readers Digest Foundation: pp. 58, 59, 60, 61, 62, 63, 64, 65; L. L. T. Rhodes/Taurus Photos: p.
74; Martin Rotker/Taurus Photos: p. 47; Mario Ruiz Picture Group: p.
96; Andrew Sacks/Art Resource: p. 20; Larry Safhol/Taurus Photos:
p. 53; Jerome Schwartz/Art Resource: p. 18; Jean-Marie Simon/Taurus
Photos: p. 10; Frank Siteman/Taurus Photos: pp. 27, 32, 35, 43; Students
Against Drunk Driving: p. 91; Szep/Boston Globe: p. 69; Taurus Photos: cover; UPI/Bettmann Newsphotos: pp. 22, 44, 66, 72, 78, 86; B.
Vatz/Taurus Photos: p. 88; Wasserman/L.A. Times Syndicate: p. 81;
Shirley Zeiberg/Taurus Photos: pp. 38, 89

Index

Jean McBee Knox is a writer who specializes in medicine and social issues. She is the author of *Drugs Through the Ages* in Series 2 of the Encyclopedia of Psychoactive Drugs, published by Chelsea House. Her articles have appeared in the *Boston Globe*, the *Globe Sunday Magazine*, the *Christian Science Monitor*, and other publications. A graduate of Wheaton College and Wesleyan University, she has taught English in Greenwich, Connecticut, and Winchester, Massachusetts.

Solomon H. Snyder, M.D., is Distinguished Service Professor of Neuroscience, Pharmacology and Psychiatry at The Johns Hopkins University School of Medicine. He has served as president of the Society for Neuroscience and in 1978 received the Albert Lasker Award in Medical Research. He has authored *Uses of Marijuana, Madness and the Brain, The Troubled Mind, Biological Aspects of Mental Disorder,* and edited *Perspective in Neuropharmacology: A Tribute to Julius Axelrod.* Professor Snyder was a research associate with Dr. Axelrod at the National Institutes of Health.

Barry L. Jacobs, Ph.D., is currently a professor in the program of neuroscience at Princeton University. Professor Jacobs is author of *Serotonin Neurotransmission and Behavior* and *Hallucinogens: Neurochemical, Behavioral and Clinical Perspectives.* He has written many journal articles in the field of neuroscience and contributed numerous chapters to books on behavior and brain science. He has been a member of several panels of the National Institute of Mental Health.

Joann Ellison Rodgers, M.S. (Columbia), became Deputy Director of Public Affairs and Director of Media Relations for the Johns Hopkins Medical Institutions in Baltimore, Maryland, in 1984 after 18 years as an award-winning science journalist and widely read columnist for the Hearst newspapers.